## Praise for *Fear and Other Stories*

"With these nine stunning—and stunningly rendered—stories by the Yiddish modernist Chana Blankshteyn, Anita Norich demonstrates yet again the power of feminist translation as cultural salvage in the face of erasure and amnesia."

—Naomi Seidman, Chancellor Jackman Professor
of the Arts, University of Toronto

"Anita Norich's vivid, nuanced translations and illuminating introduction offer an important recovery project: the work of a forgotten Yiddish woman modernist, whose riveting stories explore the fracturing impact of historical crises (WWI, the Russian Revolution and Civil War, the rise of Nazism) on everyday life. Life-affirming despite the horror, she explores the sense of community in a Jewish urban courtyard in Vilnius and collaborative work in a Paris fashion salon. In terse prose, we enter the thoughts of a Jewish woman mathematician, a medical researcher, and the revolutionary granddaughter of a Hasidic rabbi."

—Chana Kronfeld, Bernie H. Williams Professor of Comparative,
Hebrew and Yiddish Literature, UC Berkeley

"This is a remarkable collection of stories that speaks to important themes in Yiddish literature and interwar literature more broadly: panic and desperation, poverty, women's education and professionalization, women's vulnerability in romantic relationships, and the intersection of hope and hypocrisy. The volume is a significant contribution to the field because of the dearth of translations of women who wrote in Yiddish and the growing, valiant impetus to champion their writing. These stories give us a window into the immediate prewar moment, one that is often described and remembered through the lens of the catastrophic events that followed."

—Jessica Kirzane, editor-in-chief of *In geveb*

"Reading as a translator, it is usually tempting to pick up the Yiddish every few paragraphs, peer at a word choice, and try to trace the seams. But in Norich's hands, Blankshteyn's stories are so smooth, their diction so inevitable, as to constitute that elusive achievement: 'a second original.'"

—Miriam Udel, editor and translator, *Honey on the Page:*
*A Treasury of Yiddish Children's Literature*

"With a delicate and magical pen, Blankshteyn shows us men and women living through tumultuous times. Translator Anita Norich has rescued a treasure."

—Ellen Cassedy, author of *We Are Here: Memories of the Lithuanian Holocaust*

"Anita Norich's sensitive translations bring Blankshteyn's artful voice to a new generation of readers. Blankshteyn's stories are alive with the cosmopolitan worlds of interwar Jewish life, vibrating with energy and possibility against the tense backdrop of war and revolution in Europe. In them we find deeply personal expressions of Jewish modernity: a Soviet official marries the granddaughter of a Hasidic rebbe in a secret religious ceremony; a young mathematician loses herself in a reverie replete with nymphs and sprites; and the daughter of a Parisian artist model, abandoned by her mother, becomes the head seamstress in a fashion atelier, seeking love and family. These tales, first published on the eve of the Nazi invasion of Poland, offer a unique view of European Jewry from the pen of a talented woman writer."

—Allison Schacter, associate professor of English and Jewish studies, Vanderbilt University, author of *Women Writing Jewish Modernity, 1919–1939*

"From the frontlines of war and revolution to a Paris salon and the social complexities of an Eastern European Jewish courtyard, the rediscovery of Chana Blankshteyn expands our vision with stories from the interwar Yiddish press that shocked and moved readers in her own time, and now in our own. *Fear and Other Stories* joins a growing list of translations that challenge and expand our understanding of modern Yiddish literature. Anita Norich has been at the forefront of the necessary rereading."

—Justin Cammy, professor of world literatures, Smith College

"Chana Blankshteyn presents us with a range of characters in the midst of the tumultuous decades preceding the Second World War. Seemingly simple stories take unexpected turns. Anita Norich's superb translation unravels a masterly writer."

—Monika Adamczyk-Garbowska, professor of comparative literature, Maria Curie-Sklodowska University in Lublin, Poland

# FEAR

### AND **OTHER STORIES**

# FEAR
## AND OTHER STORIES

Chana Blankshteyn

*Translated by Anita Norich*

WAYNE STATE UNIVERSITY PRESS
DETROIT

ISBN 978-0-8143-4927-4 (paperback)
ISBN 978-0-8143-4928-1 (hardcover)
ISBN 978-0-8143-4929-8 (e-book)

Library of Congress Control Number: 2021951001

Wayne State University Press rests on Waawiyaataanong, also referred to as Detroit, the ancestral and contemporary homeland of the Three Fires Confederacy. These sovereign lands were granted by the Ojibwe, Odawa, Potawatomi, and Wyandot Nations, in 1807, through the Treaty of Detroit. Wayne State University Press affirms Indigenous sovereignty and honors all tribes with a connection to Detroit. With our Native neighbors, the press works to advance educational equity and promote a better future for the earth and all people.

Wayne State University Press
Leonard N. Simons Building
4809 Woodward Avenue
Detroit, Michigan 48201-1309

Visit us online at wsupress.wayne.edu.

# Contents

# Introduction

E verything about this collection of nine stories, originally written in Yiddish, is remarkable, including the fact that it exists at all. It was published just weeks before the Nazis invaded Poland and undertook what came to be known as the Final Solution. This is not a work of Holocaust literature: there are no death camps, ghettos, partisans, victims, or survivors of the Second World War. But antisemitism is palpable, as is the threat of war and its aftermath. What could it have felt like to live under these conditions? How might a woman, a feminist, a Jew, an activist—all of the things Chana Blankshteyn (1860?–1939) herself was—understand the recent past of war and revolution through which she lived and also confront what was beginning to unfold? The stories in this volume first appeared in the periodical press, but the collection was published in July 1939, just two weeks before its author's death.[1] It was one of the last Yiddish books to appear in Vilna before the Second World War, and its stories are both a view of the final gasp of Eastern European Jewish culture and a compelling modern perspective on the broader world.

The contemporary English reader encounters these stories with knowledge of a history Blankshteyn could not have imagined. It is ironic to think of her death as something of a blessing that spared her from the fate of her native Vilna's Jews and let her die in her bed.

---

1. The book's flyleaf indicates that it was issued with the aid of the Vilna Jewish community and a group of the author's friends.

Yiddish literature is often subjected to such distorting retrospective views. Still in this instance they seem almost inevitable. It is, indeed, difficult to ignore the history that followed 1939—the year of this volume's Yiddish publication, of Blankshteyn's death, and of the beginning of World War II. Yet it is important to keep in mind that the German occupation in her stories takes place during World War I, not World War II.

The battles in these stories are fought between opposing sides in the civil wars that accompanied and followed the Bolshevik Revolution. Only in one story—"Director Vulman"—do we encounter the growing, though as yet unnamed, Nazi threat. The dizzying changes of jurisdiction over Blankshteyn's Vilna (Vilnius/Wilno) is always in the background—and often in the foreground—of these stories. Vilna's population was predominantly Polish and Jewish in the interwar period and there was considerable tension between Poles and Jews, but everyone was subject to the changes of rule the city endured. Vilna was, at various times, Russian, German, Lithuanian, Polish, Soviet.[2] The search for a place, the alienation and uncertainty that permeate Blankshteyn's stories, are an expression of these political realities.

•

Only two copies of Blankshteyn's book are now to be found in the United States, one at the Yiddish Book Center in Amherst, Massachusetts, and the other at YIVO (Institute for Yiddish Research) in New

---

2. Between 1795 and 1914, Vilna was part of the Russian Empire; during World War I, it came under German rule; in 1918, it was named the capital of newly independent Lithuania; in 1919, it fell under Soviet rule and was named the capital of the Lithuanian-Byelorussian Soviet Socialist Republic; a few months later, it was taken over by Poland; within a year, it was once again under Soviet jurisdiction; in 1920, it was handed over to Lithuania; by 1922, Poland claimed it once more, though Lithuania did not cede sovereignty; it was considered part of Poland until the Second World War.

York. The Book Center's copy somehow made its way from Vilna to St. Louis and then to Amherst.[3] It bears a note dated April 1940. The copy in the YIVO library includes a note dated November 1943, yet another indication of the book's survival against all odds. To have published a book in Vilna in July 1939 and have it turn up in St. Louis in 1940 and New York in 1943 is surely noteworthy. YIVO's copy was donated by Hirsz Abramowicz (1881–1960), an educator and essayist who had known Blankshteyn in Vilna and who was on a speaking tour in North America when the war broke out.[4] The Book Center's copy is dedicated to S. Karatnik of St. Louis and is signed by Anna Abramowicz. It is not clear how the books made their way to the United States. Whether Abramowicz brought a copy with him on his trip, or one or both copies were sent to him in New York or Karatnik in St. Louis in the days when mail was still possible, the books' voyages are at once a fascinating mystery and a reminder of those who could not follow their path.

Yet another serendipitous occurrence: Max Weinreich (1894–1969), the most important Yiddish linguist of the twentieth century, was also abroad (at a conference in Denmark) when the war broke out, and

3. Elaine K. Alexander, "From Dust and Dumpsters, Fans Step In to Rescue Yiddish Language Books," *St. Louis Jewish Light*, November 19, 2014, https://stljewishlight.org/news/news-local/from-dust-and-dumpsters-fans-step-in-to-rescue-yiddish-language-books/.

4. Hirsz Abramowicz published a volume of essays titled *Farshvundene geshtaltn* [Vanished figures] (Buenos Aires: Association of Polish Jews in Argentina, 1958). Max Weinreich wrote a foreword to Abramowicz's book praising the author and his work. An edited collection of these essays appeared in English: *Profiles of a Lost World: Memoirs of East European Jewish Life before World War II*, translated by Eva Zeitlin Dropkin, edited by Jeffrey Shandler and Dina Abramowicz (Detroit: Wayne State University Press, 1999). Anna Abramowicz was in Vilna in 1940 and would die in Treblinka in 1943. For more than fifty years, Dina Abramowicz was the renowned librarian at YIVO. She was the daughter of Anna and Hirsz Abramowicz and was reunited with her father in New York in 1946, having survived the war as a librarian in the Vilna ghetto, a partisan, and a member of "the paper brigade" that saved Jewish books and archival material.

also made his way to New York. Helping to establish YIVO's new home in New York, Weinreich was instrumental in laying the foundations of Yiddish study first in Europe and then in the United States. Weinreich wrote a short foreword to the book (as he would later do for fellow Vilnian Hirsz Abramowicz), another testament to the importance of Chana Blankshteyn within Eastern European Jewish culture. The foreword offers no literary analysis or biographical information. Instead, it considers the role of professional writers in the Yiddish world and praises Blankshteyn for not depending on writing for her livelihood. One may wonder if, rather than engaging with the stories, Weinreich simply agreed to add his illustrious name to the work of a dying woman whom he had known in Vilna.[5]

Chana Blankshteyn may be almost entirely forgotten now but she was widely admired during her long and productive life. Biographical information about her is scant, and one source occasionally contradicts another.[6] Born Chana (Anna/Anyuta) Shur, she was the youngest child in a well-to-do family and was educated by German and French governesses before being sent abroad to continue her studies in France and Germany. She was briefly married when she was seventeen or eighteen.

5. The cultural concerns of Blankshteyn, Weinreich, and Abramowicz often overlapped and, on at least one occasion, they shared a platform, speaking at a celebration in honor of Avrom Morevski's birthday (as reported in *Literarishe bleter*, July 30, 1937). Morevski was a well-known actor and writer who, like these other cultural figures, hailed from Vilna.

6. Biographical sources include a biography written by Hirsz Abramowicz that appeared in the *Leksikon fun der nayer yidisher literatur* (Biographical lexicon of modern Yiddish literature). (The manuscript copy of Abramowicz's biography is missing from the YIVO archives.) In English, the authoritative sources are: Ellen Kellman, "Feminism and Fiction: Khane Blankshteyn's Role in Interwar Vilna," *Polin* 18 (2005): 221–39; and Ellen Kellman, "Creating Space for Women in Inter-War Jewish Vilna," in *Jewish Space in Central and Eastern Europe: Day-to-Day History*, ed. Jurgita Siauciunaite-Verbickiene and Larisa Lempertiene (Newcastle: Cambridge Scholars Publishing, 2007). See also Joanna Lisek, "Feminist Discourse in Women's Yiddish Press in Poland," in *Pardes: Zeitschrift der Vereinigung für Jüdische Studien E.V.* 10 (2010), 92–116.

Her second marriage to a rich diamond merchant with whom she had two children brought her to Kiev where she lived until her second divorce brought her back to Vilna. She lived for some (unspecified) time in Kiev and also with a married daughter in St. Petersburg around the time of World War I, when she served as a nurse in the Russian army. Impoverished, she returned to Vilna in the early 1920s. Only then did she begin to write in Yiddish, a language she learned in order to further her political and social work among Vilna's Jews. Remarkably, in her sixties and seventies she acquired a command of Yiddish that was, as these stories attest, indistinguishable from that of learned native speakers. Blankshteyn would go on to have an illustrious career in Yiddish publishing and, at her death, eulogies heralded her as a writer and a pioneer for women's rights and the poor.

In the *Leksikon fun der nayer yidisher literatur*, Abramowicz states that Blankshteyn stood for election to the Polish Sejm (parliament) though, as the critic Ellen Kellman indicates, that is unlikely. Instead, writes Kellman, she was a candidate for the Vilna city council on a Jewish women's list in 1927 and lost, and then, just months before her death, she ran again for a seat on the council (and lost) on a Poaley Tsiyon (Labor Zionist) slate.

Blankshteyn was best known for the stories in this collection and for the overlapping themes in her essays and political and social work. She adhered to the beliefs of the Folkspartey (Yiddish People's Party). Recognizing Yiddish as the language of the masses, the Folkspartey was founded in the wake of the pogroms following the 1905 Russian Revolution. It called for national cultural autonomy, asserting that Jews were an ethnic minority with a distinct secular, linguistic, and cultural identity that should be acknowledged and cultivated in the lands where they lived. By the early 1930s, Folkspartey membership had dwindled along with most of its hopes for Jewish life in Eastern Europe. Blankshteyn turned to Poaley Tsiyon, a party committed to socialist ideals and to building a national polity in Palestine.

For Blankshteyn, these commitments were inseparable from her activities on behalf of women's causes and vocational training. She was instrumental in creating Vilna's Froyen fareyn (Women's Association), founded in 1924 (and active for a decade) to address the needs of Jewish women in an increasingly economically depressed and antisemitic Poland. As a publisher, editor, and journalist, Blankshteyn defended women's rights to social, sexual, and political equality. She wrote stories and essays that were serialized in the Yiddish press and edited the journal *Di froy* (Woman). Several articles she published in *Vilner tog* (Vilna's day) are clear indications of her dedication to workers and women. In "Helft zikh aleyn" (Help yourself), for example, she offered a Marxist analysis of the alienation of labor and pointed to the unemployment and overproduction resulting from capitalist exploitation of workers.[7] In another article, she lamented the fact that Yiddish critics for the most part ignored women writers.[8] The *Vilner tog* also reported on a Yiddish conference held in London during which Blankshteyn spoke out against the international traffic in women and the economic conditions that trapped many women into prostitution.[9]

•

Before the Holocaust, Vilna was known as "the Jerusalem of Lithuania" because of its importance to the spiritual life of Eastern European Jewry and its centrality in the secular Jewish and Yiddish world. Most of the stories in this collection take place in and around Vilna, but

7. Blankshteyn, "Helft zikh aleyn," *Vilner tog*, February 19, 1926.

8. Blankshteyn, "A por sho in froyen-velt" [A few hours in women's world] *Vilner tog*, March 8, 1927. The article reports on a speech given by Sara Reyzen, a Yiddish poet, prose writer, and translator. Particularly ironic given the complaint voiced by Blankshteyn and others, critics often referred to Reyzen as the sister of her more well-known brothers, Avrom and Zalmen Reyzen.

9. Blankshteyn, "Der kamf kegn shand" [The battle against shame], *Vilner tog*, June 28, 1927.

Blankshteyn also knew France and Germany well and made them an occasional setting for her characters. Wherever they are, Jews and non-Jews suffer under various occupying powers and many are caught up in the revolutionary fervor that promised much and took away almost everything. The young women in Blankshteyn's stories insist on their independence, on equality with their lovers, on meaningful labor. They vary in their occupations and their status: mathematicians, scientists, writers, fashion designers, peddlers, maids, mothers. Women are no different from men in the stories in their desire to study, work, and love.

Readers of these stories will encounter a range of intertexts Blankshteyn often seems to adapt for the Eastern European Jewish milieu that is her primary subject. One such intertext—Shakespeare's *Midsummer Night's Dream*—is apparent in the story "Do Not Punish Us." It is nearly impossible to read any of these stories without thinking of Marx (1818–83), Kafka (1883–1924), and Freud (1856–1939), whose lives and works were coterminous with hers. Nor is it possible to ignore a comparison with Isaac Babel (1894–1940), who also wrote at the same time as Blankshteyn and about the same civil wars and revolutionary upheavals.[10] Blankshteyn's use of free indirect discourse—the narrative movement into and out of a character's consciousness—presented in most cases without quotation marks, produces an effect of deep interiority. A literary device used by writers as diverse as Goethe (1749–1832) and Austen (1775–1817) and developed most famously by Flaubert (1821–80), free indirect discourse may

---

10. Max Weinreich published Yiddish translations of Freud in the mid-1930s. Kafka was translated into Yiddish by the Warsaw critic Melekh Ravitch in 1920. The work of Marx and Engels was also readily available in Yiddish. Although Blankshteyn could have read them all in German, early Yiddish translations of their work point to their importance to modern Yiddish culture. Babel's East European readers would have read him in Russian, but he, too, was translated into Yiddish. (Babel, who was fluent in Yiddish, translated Sholem Aleichem into Russian.)

remind the English reader of Virginia Woolf's novels (1882–1941) and the Yiddish reader of Dovid Bergelson's (1884–1952), both of them also her contemporaries. She was likely familiar with the works of all these writers.

Blankshteyn expresses the fracturing of time, the dehumanization and fragmentation brought about by war and upheaval, not only thematically but stylistically as well. These stories are replete with ellipses, sentence fragments, compound sentences lacking conjunctions. Uncertainty about identity abounds. Characters are often unnamed, or their names appear midstory (as, for example, in "The First Hand" and "The Decree"). They may refer to themselves in the third person (as in "Director Vulman" and "The Decree"). Only one story—"Our Courtyard"—is narrated in both the first person and the present tense. Physical descriptions of places are especially vivid, as if to counter the realization that these characters cannot be grounded anywhere. We find detailed, often lyrical views of nature—trees, flowers, vegetables—but also of buildings, streets, courtyards, the marketplace. Everyday things and nature are anthropomorphized: a yawning clock in "The First Hand," a breathing car at the beginning of "The Decree," a curious moon in "An Incident," shuddering poplars gazing longingly into the water in "Who?" Synecdoche in these stories points to the impossibility of achieving wholeness or completeness. A man is introduced as "a dark beard" ("Who?"); soldiers are reduced to steel helmets ("An Incident"); a boy is "a red head of hair" ("Our Courtyard"). As in Dickens's *Hard Times*, workers are referred to as "hands" and there is a hierarchy among those who begin as lowly "third hands" and work their way up to "first hand" in the story of that name. Frame narratives abound, with past and present tenses often blurring into one another. These familiar literary devices are an analogue to the stories' themes, and their cumulative effect accentuates the uncertainties besetting all the characters.

The situations in which these characters find themselves may be

unfamiliar, but their reactions to the turmoil, the frighteningly changing times, the desire for love and self-expression are evocative and
resonant. The entrapment in "Fear," like the disbelief and horror with
which the rising German antisemitism of the 1930s is met in "Director
Vulman," or the claustrophobia of "Our Courtyard," is a quite under-
standable response to the turmoil of the first decades of the twentieth
century, but certainly not limited to those years. Similarly familiar to
the modern reader is the insistence on meaningful work for women
in "Do Not Punish Us" and "Colleague Sheyndele," and the (successful) quest to combine love and labor in "The First Hand." Men and
women delight in the physical world and in their bodies. Discreetly,
but unequivocally, Blankshteyn makes it clear that sexual desire and
lovemaking do not depend on marriage. Sometimes men betray or
objectify women. In "Who?" a deceiving fiancé dupes a young woman
into having sex with him, asserting he is going into battle and fears he
will die. The kiss forced upon Colleague Sheyndele leads to an enig-
matic ending. Director Vulman has both wife and mistress, neither
of whom he regards as his equal. On the other hand, Andrée and her
lover in "The First Hand," among other characters, are committed to
one another and to their work. Both male and female protagonists in
these stories view work as their "only sovereign."

Blankshteyn's characters struggle to find their place in the world.
For most of them, this is a quite literal existential quest as they seek a
place to hide or live during periods in which governments, armies,
and borders change abruptly. The first sentences of "An Incident" offer
a succinct view of what little difference these changes make for those
with no place at all: "This morning, control of the city once again
changed hands. One set of occupiers retreated, another took over, but it
didn't make much of an impression. People were used to such changes.
In a few days the steel helmets would surely return." For those living
under such conditions, alienation is not a trope or even primarily a
philosophical or psychological state, but rather a political reality: they

are aliens in their own homes. Many of the characters seem disaffected and estranged, and Blankshteyn is at some pains to make it clear that, in this regard, there is little difference between Jews and others. Thuggish German occupiers are virulently antisemitic, but they do not discriminate between Jews and Christians when they murder people in "Director Vulman." The Jews of "The First Hand" know that their ancestors had to hide their identities during and after the Inquisition, but in the socialist world order to come, all will live as equals.

There are also explicitly Jewish themes in most of these stories. In "Our Courtyard," for example, the seasons and the cycle of Jewish holidays measure the passage of time. And, in keeping with the teachings of Poaley Tsiyon to which Blankshteyn herself turned, the story abruptly embraces the belief that the best path for Jews to follow is the one leading to Zion. In "The Decree," we encounter a young woman who will not break with tradition and insists on having a rabbi officiate at her wedding despite the Soviet injunction against marriages performed as religious rites. The proud Jewish communist she loves sees such rituals as backward and the product of a "bourgeois mentality," yet in the end he accedes to the woman and to Jewish law. The severe, often dangerous dictates of Soviet and authoritarian powers are criticized here and elsewhere, but adherence to socialist and Jewish commitments are not. Nor are they at odds with one another in Blankshteyn's stories, just as they were not at odds in her life's work. Ultimately, these commitments offer a view of the things worth sustaining and the things that must be changed. They also point to the work that must be done.

# A Note about the Translation

These stories were published under the title *Noveles* (novellas). I have changed that title and the sequence of the stories for the English reader who is less familiar than Blankshteyn's Yiddish readers would have been with the events of the period and with the author herself. *Noveles*' table of contents lists the stories in the following order:

*Director Vulman*
*Fear*
*Do Not Punish Us*
*The First Hand*
*Colleague Sheyndele*
*Who?*
*The Decree*
*Our Courtyard*
*An Incident*

Changing the title of the collection to *Fear and Other Stories* and placing "Fear" first underscores the feeling of many of these stories' characters and, I suspect, its readers as well. Although near the end of "Fear" there is "clarity," readers may be understandably unclear about what that can mean in this context. Despite everything, the protagonist feels "the awesome power of life" and understands "the enormous, singular value of *being*, of naked being." The word "fear" appears frequently throughout this collection, but so does the desire to *be* despite that fear.

Yiddish incorporates, adapts, is influenced by, and often revels in the inclusion of lexical and syntactic elements from the languages among which its speakers live. One would be hard-pressed to find a Yiddish writer or reader who was not, like Blankshteyn herself, multilingual. There are traces of that polyglossia in her stories, but they are (thankfully, for the translator!) less frequent than one might expect from someone who lived in multiple languages. She uses words of Slavic, German, and Hebrew derivation that her readers would have simply understood as part of Yiddish vocabulary. Rather than distinguish between such words as *byuro* and *kantor*, to take only one example—the first derived from German and the second from Russian or Lithuanian—I translate both as "office" because that is how Vilna's Yiddish readers would have understood them. At times, particularly in "Do Not Punish Us," Blankshteyn transliterates words of Greek or Latin derivation that are unknown or even more rare in Yiddish than in English (*kirasn* for cuirassers, *kavalern* for cavaliers, *gnomen* for gnomes, *nymphen* for nymphs, *satir* for satyr; also *heteres* for hetaera in "The First Hand"). I have included and glossed for the English reader the few instances of Polish or Russian in the text (*sokol, Pani, pretch, vosmey dyesyatnik*). Words from French or German (*Fräulein, adieu, meine Herrn*) indicate an educated or, perhaps, affected mode of speech and I assume that, like Blankshteyn's Yiddish readers, English readers will understand them as such. I have translated or glossed many of the names of Jewish holidays, months, and rituals that may be unfamiliar to the English reader. But I have also left more readily accessible words (shtetl, latkes, mazel tov, Sukkos, minyan) as a reminder of these stories' contexts.

Often the Yiddish word *yid* is translated as "man" or "person," unless there is some reason to underscore that the character is a Jew. More troublesome is the question of whether to refer to a character as a goy, a non-Jew, a gentile, or simply a person. As with *yid* (Jew/man/person), I have distinguished between these various uses of *goy* depending on context. Thus, Yan (in "Our Courtyard") is referred to as "our goy" as a sign of his lowly status and the condescension or outright disdain with which he is regarded by the courtyard's Jewish inhabitants. But in other cases *goy* does not carry such a sting and I use "gentile" to indicate that the character is not part of the Jewish community. Similarly, I have translated *shabbes* as Sabbath when it refers to a Jewish custom or observance and as Saturday when it does not.

Blanskshteyn is not consistent in her punctuation. Only a few of the stories use quotation marks. Internal monologues, and even dialogues, are more often indicated by dashes and/or colons, as was customary for many of her contemporaries. Instead of smoothing out all such grammatical inconsistencies, I have reproduced many of them in the hope this may allow readers to experience at least a trace of the feelings of estrangement and discomfiture that abound in these stories.

# Max Weinreich's Foreword to the Yiddish Collection

U ntil a generation or two ago there were no professional authors among us. This was unmistakably true during the time of the Jewish Enlightenment: Perl was a merchant, Ettinger was a doctor, Aksenfeld was a notary.[1] But even among our Classicists there were two—Mendele and Peretz—who were not professional writers in the sense of earning their living from writing, and we know that even Sholem Aleichem only became one after he was able—by the skin of his teeth—to get out of doing other work.[2] Only in the generation after the Classicists did professional writers arise among Jews. Nowadays this has become the norm—if not in practice, then at least in theory.

It is no doubt a good thing when the literature of a *folk* can support its literati. But it may actually be the opposite that is true. It is not good when people of the pen are busy with other work just because they have no alternative. But it is certainly an advantage when there are writers whose gaze is directed at practical life and whose writing is secondary to that. They do not write because they must in order to

1. Josef Perl (1773–1839); Shloyme Ettinger (1802–56); Yisroel Aksenfeld (1787–1866). These men were among the earliest writers in Yiddish inspired by the Haskalah (Jewish Enlightenment).

2. The "Classicists" refers to the three most famous modern writers of Yiddish literature: Sh. Y. Abramovitsh, who created the figure of Mendele the Book Peddler (1835–1917); Shalom Rabinovitch, better known by his pen name, Sholem Aleichem (1859–1916); and I. L. Peretz (1852–1915).

make a living, but rather because they think they have something to say. The life experiences expressed in such works may sometimes be greater, more multifaceted, than in works by writers whose function it is to observe solely for the sake of writing.

Chana Blankshteyn, whose work now makes its debut before a larger audience, is one of those writers I have tried to characterize here. Vilna knows her through essays or short stories she occasionally publishes in local newspapers, but she does not publish a lot: if she has nothing to say, she remains silent. Now, at the behest of her friends, she has collected her stories into one volume. I am certain this book will be received "with a pleasant countenance."[3]

*M. Weinreich*
*Vilna, June 21, 1939*

---

3. Weinreich uses the Hebrew phrase *sever panim yafot*. The expression comes from the Talmud (Pirke Avot 1:15): "speak little, but do much, and receive all people with a pleasant countenance."

# Fear

The last stop before the final station, said someone in the narrow corridor that ran through the railroad car. A sleepy voice responded,—There's a place to eat here.—These words were swallowed up in a great big yawn.

The traveler, who lay near a window in the compartment, shook off his nap, stretched out an arm, took the train's itinerary from the table, turned the pages, and found the station. The train stays at this stop for fifteen minutes before heading off. So he figured it really was worth it to drink some tea here. That way, he wouldn't have to worry about getting his breakfast later. He could leave his suitcase at the depot and as soon as he arrived, he'd go into town. He'd be able to get all his business done quickly: see the factory owner and the people in the two banks where he had to settle a few pressing matters.

Who knows, maybe I'll manage to go back home today, he thought cheerfully and went out into the corridor.

The train drew closer to the station. From afar, the low, long station appeared. The traveler went down to the platform. It was March. A cold early morning. From the sandy plains around the station a sharp wind, blown by the nearby sea, blew the snow around so that last year's short, spiky grass seemed to be covered in dirty salt.

The traveler put his collar up and greedily breathed in the bracing air. He went quickly over some rails and into the station's buffet. The large room was empty except for two train clerks who were sitting at a table drinking beer. Clearly, they had been there a long time. Near the buffet, an older woman in a white kerchief leaned her head on her high, laced-up bosom.

The traveler, looking at the plates of sliced, dried rolls covered in sausage or cheese, frowned, and asked about tea.

—This early there's no tea prepared. But coffee?

—Coffee? Sure, please give me a glass of coffee.

The guest rubbed his cold hands together. The woman fussed over a large kettle under a stitched cover and handed over a glass of boiling hot coffee, sliding over a plate with oblong bagels.

Rushing footsteps were heard going past the door. The traveler put down his empty glass, hurried, waited impatiently for the woman to take change out of the register, ran quickly from the room, past the rails, stopping for a moment as a locomotive went by, and returned to his platform. The train started moving, the wheels turning sluggishly. His compartment was at the front. He sprang up on the steps of the nearest car, grabbed onto its handle and pulled. The handle did not move. So he leaned his shoulder against the door, pulling with all his might. The door did not budge. It was locked.

Meanwhile the wheels went faster, as if gaining strength with every rotation. At the closed car, the man pressed his fist around the brass knob and started banging on the window with his free hand. Banged and called out. Wondered why a car had been locked up in the middle of the journey. Got mad.

—Have you ever heard of such a thing!—The wind grew stronger, raised the hair on his bare head, hid behind his collar like a thief in a poorly secured apartment, moved further and further down his spine. A cold sweat covered his forehead, pouring over his cheeks. It felt as if the heavy drops were about to freeze, covering his face in an icy bark.

—Open, open already! Don't you hear? A traveler is knocking! A tra-ve-ler left behind!

The train moved over the desolate, still wintry landscape. The cars were running apace.—Let me in! Open up! What are you thinking?

I can't hold on anymore! Open!—Suddenly, a wild thought came into his head: maybe the car is empty and no one can hear him? He's screaming for nothing. For nothing, he's screaming. He's in front of a closed, empty car!

His knees were weak. A disgusted shudder went up his leg. Fear froze his limbs. With great effort, he bent his shoulders and fell with his face against the window. In the narrow entryway there was nothing to be seen. Empty. But the narrow windowpane, clouded in morning dew, reflected his dimmed eyes and his hair which wind and fear had made stand on his forehead. And at the same time a face appeared in the window. A round, childlike face above a soldier's collar was looking at him.

—Open, Open! Help!—the traveler started yelling again.

The soldier was startled, stepped back, picked up his rifle, and aimed the steel barrel at the person at the window.

Like wild beasts, the train cars threw themselves from side to side, banged, whined, their wheels beating out a tune: tar-tar-ara-ra. . . . And maybe it was he, the person at the locked door, continuously hammering with his fist on the door? The sounds drilled into his brain, screwed themselves into the marrow of his bones, roared in his ears, filled the air. Tar-tar-ara-ra. . . .

Step by step, weapon pointed toward the window, the soldier retreated. Disappeared.

The traveler startled, felt a terrible coldness in the hand holding onto the door handle. The iron bit into his skin. The palms hurt and burned. The fingers were paralyzed. The arm, the hand became limbs unto themselves, stopped obeying, lost their connection to the rest of the body. The hand could no longer connect the body to the iron grip in front of him. The hand refused to tolerate the burning of the frozen metal. In a moment it would tear itself away from the door. The man would fall. . . .

Despair took hold of the man on the step of the locked car. The despair came from somewhere deep within. The man understood it was not only the frighteningly harsh wind that raised the hair on his head. It was also fear. The blind, wild terror of dying, of not being. . . . With strange clarity, he saw before his eyes his nearest and dearest. Like a portrait, in full measure, they stood before him, and near them he saw himself, strong, energetic. A cry of woe tore out of his breast: remembering—he had read it somewhere—that only in the greatest danger does a person see with such clarity that which is dearest to him in the world. . . . He understood—it was his soul, sensing its defeat, crying within him. His heart was dying.

A soldier with stripes on his shoulders approached the window. Behind him was the young man with the childlike face, rifle at his side. The sergeant's serious, severe glance took in the cheeks, made blue by the wind, the wide-open eyes, the open mouth, screaming, begging.

—Open!

The sergeant bent closer to the window to see if there was anyone else near the man screaming at the door. A quick, sharp glance, and the hand that lay on the open holster of the pistol unlatched the door, grabbed the man's shoulders, yanked him inside. The traveler fell helplessly to the floor, landed on his knees, stood up, fell back against the wall, closed his eyes.

—Why are you trying so hard to get into a car with prisoners? Who are you looking for here?

The traveler explained, barely getting the words out, unable to stop the shivering of his lips.

—Show your passport, your papers!

—In the other car, in my suitcase!

—Come!

The fingers, which were still gripping him, biting into his arm like pliers, pushed him. The soldier with the rifle followed them. In the car, the agitated prisoners pressed against one another, among them a few intellectuals, a man in glasses with a small, pointed beard, others, all pale, everyone's eyes full of curiosity, hope, disappointment. . . .

They passed through a few cars, into the compartment. The sergeant searched for the passport, looked around, smiled.

—You're lucky this one—pointing with his head at the young soldier—didn't shoot you. Thought it was an attack. Actually, we all thought there would be an attack on the car in order to free a few prisoners.—He left hurriedly.

No one was in the compartment. The traveler sat down and leaned back in his seat. His head buzzed, his temples hammered.

Out of the noise, clarity emerged, the consciousness of the awesome power of life grew. With every limb and all his senses, he understood the value, the enormous, singular value of *being*, of naked being. . . .

# Do Not Punish Us

group of doctors, mathematicians, and lawyers who had just completed their final exams celebrated by organizing a friendly gathering. In the morning they took a boat out to a small summering place famous for its historic castle and its large, lush park stretching for several miles along the river. There was a small pavilion done in an antique Italian style, with a restaurant inside. Once upon a time, after a stroll, lovely, proud ladies with powdered hair and laced bodices rested there. Cavalrymen, and black cuirassiers, and dragoons in clothing embroidered with gold and silver drank burgundy from ladies' silk shoes, rode horses at breakneck speed, and tortured their slaves nearly to death in order to give their beloved, at the exact right moment, a note on perfumed rose paper with a royal coat of arms.

The long narrow table was set on the green meadow, encircled by old bushy fir trees and tall hundred-year-old oaks. Squirrels with golden red tails were on the branches. One could imagine that, from behind a large tree two people holding hands could not have encircled, a satyr with goat's feet might appear, looking at a wood nymph he desired.

About twenty people were sitting around the table, among them a few older friends who lived in the city. Quite a few bottles had already been emptied and lay on the grass. The group was heated by several glasses of wine, happy that the difficult months had passed and excited to be in the crystal-clear air with its strong scent of earth and trees.

She was sitting at the end of the table, refreshing herself with frozen punch. Slowly, with a small spoon, she snacked on the cold, sweet dish, and with closed eyes breathed in the strong scent of rum.

"Pretty Max" stood up from his place next to his friend, the private tutor, and approached her with measured steps. "A hot day," he said most earnestly, and waited for an answer. Pretty Max dealt with everything in the world most earnestly, and most of all with himself. A young man without uncertainties: he never doubted he would become a famous gynecologist and travel around in his own car; never doubted that all the female students were in love with him. He even pitied them a bit—clearly, he couldn't love all the women at the same time!

Since she remained silent, he moved a chair next to her, sat down and stretched out one foot in its lavender sock, exactly the same color as his enormously wide handkerchief in the breast pocket of his elegant brown summer suit. Because Pretty Max took everything so earnestly, everything about him was exaggerated: not simply well dressed, but elegant; not simply speaking, but orating—impressing even himself. Friends used to laugh at him, but in a good-natured way. To tell the truth, he never injured anyone by word or deed. The female students also laughed at him, but not really wholeheartedly—he was, after all, a handsome young man. Unusually handsome.

—I want to visit you before we all go our separate ways. Tomorrow at two o'clock I will have the honor to do so.

His brown velvety eyes claim her attention. She feels them on her skin, on her suddenly dry lips. It isn't the first time she blushes when he speaks to her. She jokes about him just like the others do, but still she likes him. Raised in her grandfather's well-to-do household in the village, she is drawn to him with all her healthy youthfulness. Whenever she meets him, her blood pulses faster and her heart beats louder. She thinks he has the same effect on the other girls. They don't want to admit it, or they just don't say so aloud.

Pretty Max stands up.

—So, tomorrow at two o'clock. You won't be bored—he continues with ingenuous solemnity. His velvety eyes caress her. A bit of red pours over her cheeks, flares down her neck. She bows her head.

—Good.

Pretty Max returns to his place near the private tutor. He is calm and earnest.

It has become very hot. And she is tired. She wants to lie down. At least for a quarter of an hour. Not more. With gentle, womanly gracefulness she stands up, takes her coat from among the clothing strewn about, and goes to sit under the trees. A friend calls. Someone laughs. She doesn't stop. She pretends not to hear.

In the woods it's not as hot. Here, under the old fir tree whose branches hang down to the ground, she stretches out. She sees them all from afar, but here it's not as noisy. The thick branches swallow the cheerful voices.

She puts her coat under her head and stretches her limbs. How nice it is here! An isolated, hidden corner. Over her head—an entwined green roof. It's just like the old story about the beautiful queen whose husband, the woodland king, cast a spell over her. She had seen illustrations of the story at the dentist's where she lived. She doesn't remember why and how the mean king cursed his wife. Her head is spinning. . . . But in such an old thick forest there really could once have been all sorts of beings, good and bad spirits, nymphs and monsters. Only now does she feel how very tired she is. Deep in her bones, she still feels the weight of the last difficult exams. The professor drove the students hard. He had been especially angry today. Maybe he was on the verge of an attack of gallstones. Whenever that happens, he doesn't know what to do with himself or others. She is not at all afraid of mathematics, but it's still good to know that everything went well. She can finally sleep peacefully. . . . But what's so strange? He? Pretty Max?

Dry needles from the fir tree pour down. Someone is coming. . . . Who can it be? Who? The tall trees move apart, the woodland king appears. Two pairs of gnomes, one pair following the other, carry his long green beard. In their free hands they hold tiny golden axes. Behind them walks the chief marshal, the old satyr with goat's feet. The woodland king, with the yellow face of the mathematics professor, stops. She wants to flee, but behind her the satyr's horns emerge. He raises his scepter with its head of a dead owl. She feels faint. She feels his green beard on her cheeks. She knows—it is a great honor when the lord of the field and forest casts his eye upon a mortal girl, but, still, she has taken all her exams. . . . Why does she deserve this! No, no!

Suddenly the branches start to rustle, thousands of birds sing sweetly, the entire meadow is full of nymphs and sprites. They stand around the woodland queen. Golden hair bedecks her white back, redolent flowers encircle her body. On her head she carries a crown of diamonds the gnomes dug out of the depths of the mountains for her. She raises her hand.

—Aha. Caught! Lusting after a young nymph!

Her mother-of-pearl bosom rises and all the birds emit a melodic sigh. The chief marshal lowers his horns and hides behind the king.

The girl under the tree jumps up on a wide tree branch. The thick growth hides her. No one sees her. The woodland king raises his nose, just like the professor.

—Foolish woman, are you jealous? Do you concern yourself with the women who creep around on the earth? They are born and disappear like dust under our feet. Don't you know I cannot allow our godly generation to die out? Even you, immortal women, do not understand your men!

A wild storm erupts. Tall trees bow down and leaves tremble. Thunder splits the sky. All the living beings fall down. The woodland king's eyes burn like fire and his voice is louder than the thunder.

—Go, foolish woman. Because of your jealous curiosity I cast upon you my royal curse. Go!

The queen lowers her head. A bejeweled tear falls from her

diaphanous eyes. She departs slowly. Around her is her frightened retinue.

The golden axes resound in the hands of the gnomes. The earth shakes under the woodland king's heavy steps. He disappears.

As soon as the godly pair disappear the thunder is silenced, the birds once again praise the day, and the sun in the clear heavens smiles down on the world.

She jumps down from the tree branch and heads through the forest. A clear river beckons her from afar. Heatedly, she throws herself into the cool stream, jumps out, dries herself in the golden sand on the shore, weaves a crown, and adorns herself with white lilies. A sweet melody is heard: the little lonesome shepherd is playing on his fife. She runs over, taps him on the forehead and hides among the bushes. But the shepherd finds her. She sits on a fallen tree trunk. She refreshes herself with the redolent honey of a green leaf that has stolen out of the hollow of an oak tree.

An old black billy goat gathers the white sheep. He knows that as soon as the young shepherd runs after a girl, he—the old billy goat—must guard the flock.

Suddenly two white doves fly by. They are blowing on narrow silver trumpets—the queen's messengers are summoning her nymphs. She remembers that she, too, is in the king's retinue. She runs to where the silver trumpets beckon.

The entire court is already assembled on the flowery meadow. In the middle stands a tall brown jackass. Its coat shines like copper under the sun. The queen rises from her throne, the white swans at her feet spread their wings and fly after her. Two nymphs bring a wreath of roses. The queen puts it on the jackass's forehead. It turns around, looks at her with big brown eyes, stretches out its head and emits a long, dreadful cry. The queen is delighted.

—Listen to how majestic and grand is his sweet voice. Listen!

Her sapphire eyes shine, her dainty hand with the coral nails stretch out. A contented sigh raises the buds on her mother-of-pearl breast. The evening stars of her crown, a gift from her sister the Night Queen, descend. Tenderly she embraces the ass's thick mane. . . .

The queen's companions cover their faces with their hair and weep quietly. Others laugh. Behind the trees there are all sorts of creatures who live in the forest and make fun of their ruler whom the king, her husband, punished with the curse that she would bless an ass with her divine body. The old satyr, the chief marshal, leans on his scepter with its head of a dead owl. He shakes his horns gleefully.

—Ha ha, the proud and beautiful queen is in love with a jackass.

The young woman under the tree trembles in sadness and pity. Shame has turned her face red. Frightened, she startles. Where is that laughter coming from? She leans on her hand. Where is she? And where is the angry woodland king with the professor's yellow face? And who is there on the meadow? She stares. A tall man is standing near the table. She sees him through the branches. His straight, dark hair falls over his ears. His brown suit glistens like a pelt. Who is he? Whom does he resemble? And why are they laughing around the table? Oh my, whom does he resemble?

The strong healthy young woman, the mathematician who graduated first in her class, sits under the bushy fir tree and sways, just like her old grandmother at home used to do when saying her prayers on the Sabbath. Swaying and murmuring and wringing her hands.

—Protect and shield me, Master of the Universe! Do not let my foolish infatuation crown the ass in my heart. Grant mercy to your daughters. Do not punish us with a jackass.

Cheerful voices call out:

—How much longer will you sleep? Get up, we're going swimming!

# The First Hand

## I

t wasn't easy for her to get the title of "first hand" in an elegant Parisian fashion salon. Her mother, well known in artist circles as a lovely model—especially among young painters who used to come to Paris to be educated—left for a movie studio in Morocco. In those days, her mother's reputation as a model kept declining. Her thin, gorgeous body became heavier. Often, she had posed as an Olympian goddess or a hetaera, but her body had lost its ideal, classical lines. As a result, the no-longer young woman gladly agreed to pose for popular pictures of Oriental scenes.

Little Andrée never saw her mother again. Disappeared. Vanished. In the studio's office they said she had remained somewhere in Tunis. Nothing more was known about her.

Andrée never knew her father. A small, framed painting hung on the wall of their home. Once, in the summer, when the painters left on vacation and her mother couldn't pay the rent, the caretaker came up to their fourth-floor apartment. The ugly, dried-up woman had never behaved kindly to her beautiful mother, who constantly laughed and joked with the cheerful young artists. The caretaker yelled and said she would throw them out of the house. Her mother answered. Both women screamed. It was in the morning. The argument woke the child. She jumped out of bed and tearfully held on to her agitated, upset mother. When the caretaker left, her mother took the frightened girl by the hand and led her to the painting hanging on the wall.

—I will never sell this, although if I did, I would be able to pay the rent to that witch. Your father painted it.

—Where is he, my father?

—He died. I honored his dying wish. His friends say he could have become a great painter if he hadn't died so young.

The child pointed to the painting with her little hand.

—What is that?

—An old, poor temple in your father's home, far, far away from here.

It showed men wrapped in white shawls standing in a narrow, low-ceilinged room. Through a large window off to the side a snowy white field could be seen. The sun reflected off the snow and shone into the room. Long, narrow beams spreading out from the windowpanes and mixing with the pale glow of yellow lights in tall copper candlesticks pulsated on the men's bowed white backs. A golden white haze hovered over the entire place.

The girl looked at the painting and, for the rest of her life, the thought of her unknown father was bound up with a soft, hazy whiteness. That morning a few tears flowed over her mother's pretty face, but in the evening it was once again cheerful in the small attic apartment.

The picture her father had painted was sold after a while. That happened when her mother was sick, could not pose for several months, and the cheerful young artists had to find another model.

The aunt with whom her mother left the child when she went to Morocco was a poor widow. She earned her living by serving in several houses: cleaning rooms, washing dishes, preparing supper. She was hardly home during the day, so she left the girl in a municipal orphanage. There Andrée finished the schooling she had earlier begun and learned how to sew. With the ability to adjust to every situation so typical for Parisian children of her background, she quickly got used to the monotonous, arid conditions reigning in the orphanage and forgot the sometimes hungry, sometimes sated, but always happy-go-lucky life she had led with her mother in the attic rooms in Montmartre.

For a long time, she waited for her vanished mother. With time, the image of the pretty woman slowly faded. No one spoke of her father again. Needless to say, the thought of him faded too. In the orphanage, no one asked her about her parents. Who cared who she was? Was she the only homeless, deserted child growing up in the large city of Paris?

When she turned fifteen, the director of the orphanage arranged a job for her as an errand girl in a large women's clothing business. There, on the sixth floor of a cavernous building, she slept alongside a few other homeless orphans. From morning till night, she ran from one department to another, back and forth on the stairs. She lugged materials, brought trimmings to match the colors of the clothes, cleaned up the messy tables, threaded needles, delivered pins. At midday she went out to the street to get a bite to eat for the women in her workshop. They would sometimes give her a piece of chocolate or a bit of something else. Someone always wanted the errand girl to do something. She was always on her feet.

After a few years Andrée was allowed to watch the fittings, bind materials, and sit in the workshop. The errand girl became a "third hand." She was thin and dark, with a pair of large steel-gray eyes that shone in her pale, narrow face. The shop made fine evening and ball gowns. Even at that early stage, Andrée could quickly and firmly handle the expensive, richly colored silks, separate layers of delicate lace with her thin fingers, gather clouds of lightweight tulle. The third hand understood at a glance what the first hand wanted. Now and then, the second hand would consult her about a decoration, a bow, a flower. After work, the girl was so tired and dejected she could barely wait to go to sleep.

The fashion house had an exclusive clientele, mostly from the provinces, from religious, aristocratic society, and so the business paid attention to how the girls who lived in the shop behaved. Relationships between them and the young men employed by the firm were forbidden. But Andrée was so thin and colorless, and also so preoccupied and weary, not even the elevator boys were interested in her. If someone did occasionally bother her, her strong, powerful hands did not hesitate to give a decisive push and use her sharp tongue to say some sarcastic words in the language of the streets. It was clear the young girl was the child of Parisian streets and knew about life from her earliest years on.


## II


After a few years, the business experienced a serious crisis. The number of office staff and workers was reduced. The "first" whom Andrée had served went over to an exclusive workshop for women's clothing. She took along the "third." In the new place, Andrée rose in rank: she became the second hand with a small raise. Now she could afford to live alone in a furnished room in the Latin Quarter. The house had mostly poor students, clerks, and some workers skilled in various industries and businesses.

She stayed home on Sundays, straightened out her things, patched her clothes, or sewed a dress. She loved to read. But she did not like novels. She eagerly swallowed historical works and, mostly, travel stories her neighbors lent her. On Sunday afternoons she sometimes visited her aunt, who lived in a suburb of Paris. In good weather they sat in the garden of a small worker's café on the banks of the Seine and drank a glass of lemonade. Every two weeks, without fail, she went to the Louvre's art galleries. She knew the paintings well, had friends among the magnificent beings in their heavy gilded frames.

Since Andrée showed great taste in copying styles and matching colors, she was often sent to the theater to see what the performers wore. Slowly, from the awkward thin girl emerged a slim, graceful Parisienne with healthy, clear skin and large, rather pensive steel-grey eyes.

Her friends wondered why no one came to pick her up after work. They sometimes invited her to go with them on Sunday when they went out of town. They would sail on the river, eat in the woods, or listen to some music in a restaurant. Sometimes young men whom the girls knew would come too, but such jaunts were infrequent. The group would quickly split up; the young women wanted to spend their free day with their boyfriends. But Andrée was always alone. Her friends laughed about it.

—The second thinks she's something special, so she's waiting for a nobleman.

Andrée was not offended. Her eyes smiled. She was in no hurry, had no urge yet.

The salon was steeped in an atmosphere of luxury and pleasure. The rich customers brought with them the aura of expensive perfumes, fresh flowers they kept in their cars, refined coquetry, a deep desire to be pretty, to please, to tease. . . .

Sometimes a well-dressed, well-trained athlete, or an older, sedate businessman would come to see the final fitting of a ball gown or an expensive coat. Other times an unhappy man would ask if his wife, or a friend in whom he was interested, had been to the salon or would come there that day. Or other times a woman waited eagerly for someone, telephoned, wandered around the shop, looked at clothes, studied the fashion magazines, seemed to search for a particular style, impatiently looked at the door, listened for steps in the front room. . . . The workers had their revenge, snickering: things aren't always happy even among the rich.

But their money, their leisure was enviable. The women's riches were provoking: in the morning a woman might be an athlete, almost like a slim young man, in the evening a noblewoman wrapped in fancy materials, tulle and lace, wearing pearls and colorful stones, imitation jewelry, the ostentatious stuff under which today's fashion seeks to hide the general impoverishment, the postwar European destitution. Fear of the future hid behind the reigning debauchery.

But Andrée was mostly interested in the American women who were the most numerous and best customers. She was amazed at the ease with which they spent money, taking their checkbooks out of their elegant purses. She liked their independence, their calm confidence, their relationship with men, their open, almost comradely cool flirtation, so different from what she had known. But more than anything she was jealous of their ability to travel around the world, visiting foreign places, seeing other people, other lands.

Sometimes, in the middle of work, the girl would suddenly stand lost in thought and say to herself: laboring throughout life, working so hard, she wanted nothing else, but sometime, at some later point, she wanted to be able to see the world, see that far-off land where snow glistens and the bluish fire of tall candles mingles with golden rays, see the land where that low-ceilinged building stands. A warm whiteness hovers around the white, bowed beings. . . .

In the business, it was believed that the styles and cosmetics with which a woman adorns herself, and even the sport of it all, were primarily decoration, a sort of prelude to flirtation, to love. . . . No wonder the bit of joy—the boyfriend—occupied such an important place in the lives of the female workers, a life of endless labor, the constant fight for a higher position that must be defended against experienced, energetic competitors. All week one is yoked to work and if there is finally a free day loneliness accompanies it, especially during the summer when thousands and thousands of people go on trips with their families and the grand workers' army leaves Paris.

Andrée finally managed to do as others did; for a while, she went to a nearby café with the friend of one of her neighbors. Sometimes they would go as a threesome, sometimes as a couple. A few times they ventured further, spending half a day on the banks of the river. The student was a calm, sensible, average person. He finished the university, got ready to take over his father's notary office in a small town in Normandy. If Andrée had had a dowry, a little money, any kind of support, or the backing of a family, perhaps he would have married her. He told her that. Andrée had nodded, smiled. . . .

She really liked that young man. Good not to be alone. But even if the match had been possible, the child of Paris was not attracted to life in a far-off province, surrounded by priests and small-town aunties. The worker of the worldly city could not have gotten used to the choking constraints of such a life. No, it was no good for either of them.

Meanwhile, they went walking on the broad boulevards, stopping together in front of large shop windows, just like a serene, engaged couple.

Soon the final notary exams began; soon he had to go back home. His uncle, a rural priest, wrote that he had already found a bride for his nephew, the widow of a rich, neighboring farmer. Why was he still sitting in Paris? The whole family was impatiently waiting for him. The young man left. What else could have happened? Both of them had known from the start that it had to be that way.

They said their goodbyes at the train station. The young notary was upset: maybe they were destined to see one another again sometime? "I'll write to you," he said, standing at the open window and bending toward her. "You are a strong woman, I was often afraid of you. . . ."

There was an emptiness after his departure. Some uneasiness. They were probably not destined to see one another again. A few letters, a postcard, and their correspondence was cut off. A pity. They had gotten used to one another. Well, but that's life. . . .

After a while, there was someone else: a short, banal encounter with someone in the crowded underground metro. He lived in the same neighborhood where she worked, so they had seen one another from afar. They spoke. A few days later she noticed him walking by her store and looking around. Then they went out together for a while. A perfectly nice, solid man. Tried subtly to ask about her life, her family.

And then after a while, midday, coming back on the tram from a fashion show where she had gone with the first, she saw him with his arm around a small pregnant woman, guiding her slowly across the street. Andrée clearly saw his embarrassment, his stiff short greeting, and had no doubt the small woman was his wife. The girl shuddered—how ugly is the underside of life, how rotten, how vulgar.

She saw him the next day. She didn't stop, quickly disappeared in the crowd. He understood. . . .

Andrée was no longer the homeless girl who had, since childhood, been afraid she would never find a man. She no longer feared that no man would take care of her. Now she was an accomplished, intelligent worker, liked her craft, felt she had the drive and energy to move forward in life.

And love? She still remembered the turmoil, the clamor, the abuse raging on all the floors of the house where she had lived with her mother. She still saw in her mind's eye the angry scowl on the face of the caretaker who had watched her husband so carefully, jealous of every woman. She remembered the stories told by the girls in the orphanage and in the workshop. Seldom did their relationships end well. The joy of the beginning, of first blush quickly changed to unhappiness, complaints, pale faces, tearful eyes. . . . It was seldom different. And into this gray, bitter daily life would suddenly come a few gunshots, a bottle of lye, blindness, a repulsive, permanently disfigured face, suffering, despair, regret. Love? No! It was not for her. She had other things to do.

# III

Soon, something happened that changed Andrée's life. A poor, malnourished girl who had fled the Ukrainian pogroms came into her department. She was brought to the shop by a Jewish customer who was a Russian émigré. The girl quarreled with the third hand. It came to blows, with the third hand, a French girl, slapping her. When the Jewish girl tried to jump up, she slipped and fell off her chair. Some of the workers said she had fallen on purpose, others defended her. Andrée came in. She quieted them down and asked the director to punish the one who had hit the new girl. Most of the other workers agreed.

The next day the French girl was sitting at her work as if nothing had happened. She bragged about it to the second. Andrée demanded that the French girl be fired within the week. But the director did not find it necessary to defend the foreign girl who was, according to him, not entirely suitable for their shop.

That same evening Andrée left the salon. The first, who had brought her there, had gone to take care of her ailing father. No one even asked Andrée to stay. She was thought to be too proud. What was she thinking? Was there a lack of experienced, able workers in Paris, especially during the summer? The season of balls and large parties was already past. Vacation was coming soon.

At home, Andrée counted the money she had saved. Enough for two or three months. She would certainly find work in the fall. She could wait calmly. Meanwhile, she would mend her winter coat and her few clothes. But first of all, sleep, rest her bones. And then begin to look, go to the offices, ask, find something better.

And that's just how it was: rested, she went walking. Mostly in the Bois de Boulogne. She would stop at the wide, beautiful spot from which paths led in every direction. She contemplated the gorgeous landscape, looked at the cars, horseback riders, pedestrians, at all the movement reigning there in the morning. Unwittingly, instinctively, she assumed the free, confident walk of the women whom she had, until then, seen only briefly in the workshop. She wholeheartedly enjoyed the scene, which made this place into the most beautiful corner in the world. She immersed herself in the beauty of the old trees, delighted her strained eyes with the fresh greenery, breathed in the clean air, was pleased to feel the rhythmic movement of her healthy, supple body.

A few times a week, in the evening, Andrée went to art classes. She had long wanted to do that but never had the time. She could easily sketch a new style that she saw in the theater or at an exhibition in the world-renowned salons. But she lacked technical skill: how to copy the details precisely, to transfer graceful lines onto paper, to show movement. She never missed the English language courses on Saturdays. Sundays she often went to the Louvre. Now, during vacation time, the old historic building was visited more often than in winter. The French middle class, and especially the working class, loved their country's art treasures, and on Sundays entire families walked around the tall rooms of the former royal palace. Also, in the summer tourists and people from the provinces were drawn to the city.

Andrée's aunt, the housemaid, had been in the hospital since winter. She had long been ill, had a weak heart, barely dragged her swollen feet. One wet, cold evening she slipped on the stairs, fell, lay down in bed and never stood up again—had toiled enough.

One Sunday late afternoon, when Andrée came to check on her, the patient lay with her face turned to the open window, gazing at the green branches of the tall blossoming linden tree outside. . . . Andrée sat down on the chair near her bed.

—See, I'm also on vacation. Lying like a noblewoman, and the garden peers into my room.

In the large hospital expanse sat friends and acquaintances of the patients. Her aunt looked around.

—And my niece came to visit me too, just as happens among

respectable people, and she brought me good things to eat—her aunt said, thanking her for the plate of blueberries Andrée handed her.

It was quiet in the hospital. A dull, grey uneasiness hung over the white beds. The visitors listened unwillingly to the moans coming from all sides, and watched the nurse who drifted among the patients like a white shadow.

The leaves of the linden tree could be seen through the window as they murmured a sleepy tune. Her aunt dozed. After a while, she opened her eyes and said to her niece,

—You don't resemble your mother at all. You're entirely different. Thank God you don't have the beauty that ruined your mother. Our family comes from honorable workers. If your mother had remained a hardworking woman, like all of us, she would have had a husband and would perhaps still be alive. I am dying peacefully. I know you won't stray from the right path, won't forget that your grandfather fell a victim to the horrifying slaughter at the holy wall of the cemetery.

In her dying heart blazed the old enmity of the miserable and the wronged. Her flailing, dry hand caressed the girl's face.

A few days later the niece was told that her aunt had died. At the head of her bed they found a bankbook with a little money and a note about her funeral. For many years, the old, honorable woman had saved her poor earnings, wanting to be buried in her own burial shrouds.

After the small funeral for the poor old worker, Andrée felt completely alone for the first time—alone in the great big alien world.

Summer was coming to an end. It was late August and the large fashion houses were getting ready for the new season. In a month the customers would come back from the spas and beaches. Andrée had not yet found work. One employment bureau suggested she take a job in the provinces, but she did not want that: whatever there was to achieve could only be done in Paris. Despite her thriftiness and practicality, there was very little money left. She began to reflect: She had been living in the same house for quite a few years. Always paid on time, lived a respectable, quiet life and earned the trust of the caretaker, and also of the baker and merchants on their street. She could doubtless live on credit for a while. But for how long?

Now Andrée spent most of her time at home. She spared herself the cost of the tram, sat in the square, stopped her courses, practiced drawing, read books a student had left for her before going on vacation. Children played around the benches. She looked at the little ones, with bottles between their lips. Sometimes a mother would ask her to watch over a child while she ran off to buy something for her husband's supper. Andrée walked around with the baby carriage, covered the little feet that threw off their blankets, gently patted the child's little body. She made friends in the small world at the benches. Hands stretched out to her. Soft, wet, grimacing faces cried when she left. The girl thought: a child. That's something just for me. She wanted to have a child. As with most girls, the mother was awakened in her heart much earlier than the woman. For now, the woman slept.

# IV

One day, the employment bureau said there was a possibility for Andrée to get work. The bureau's director informed her,

—A new firm, started just a few years ago, had good customers. The owner had been a singer, inherited a small fortune from her uncle, was invested in the business, so she was looking for a first hand who had not just ordinary technical ability like the earlier forewoman of the workshop, but also good taste, the ability to create fresh new styles. Since the business was not rich, an unpretentious person was sought for a trial of about two months.

—Did the young lady think she would be able to take such a position?

Let her think carefully, because later, in a few months, if she was unable to satisfy these conditions, it would be the middle of the autumn season and then it would be very difficult to find other work.

Andrée lifted her eyes to the director.

—Yes, she thought she could try it.

—You should go to the shop on Monday morning. The owner will make the final decision. You're lucky you are the first to come today. If you are an energetic person, you can make something of yourself there.

The director's American eyeglasses looked her up and down, appraising her with a practiced eye.

That was on Friday. Saturday went by. Sunday dragged on like a lazy old mare sick of moving her hairy gray legs. Andrée's few friends were on vacation or away somewhere outside Paris. She was uneasy, the uneasiness of empty hours that accompany lonesome wanderers on the busy, lively streets. Her head throbbed as if hammers were hitting it. And what if nothing changed tomorrow? Her heart trembled restlessly. Today she was not in the mood to enjoy art; her hands, drab and bony from daily labor, seemed to push away the paintings and the marble figures. Instead of them, it was the unknown, dark tomorrow that appeared before her eyes. Still, in order to calm her agitated nerves, she went to the Louvre.

The high-ceilinged rooms were nearly empty. Andrée sat down on a velvet bench and gazed at all the pictures on the wall. Were they happy, those powdered ladies- and gentlemen-in-waiting, the cardinals clothed in red, the beautiful proud women?

A foreign, sonorous voice asked something in bad French. A middle-aged man politely excused himself.

—The attendant isn't here and he himself is a foreigner, wants to see the sculptures, doesn't know where to go. The Fräulein is no doubt a Parisienne, maybe she knows the way.

Andrée began to explain,—The third room on the right. After that, the gallery.

The foreigner listened attentively, but it was clear he was disoriented.

—I'll show you.—She seized the opportunity not to be alone in her present agitation.

On the way, the foreigner said he was a Spaniard, in Paris for the first time. He had made arrangements with a friend, another Spaniard, to meet here. But . . .

—Ah, here comes my friend.

A lively young man of average height approached them. His firm, broad steps did not match his slim figure and his angular, anxious face. Surprised by seeing Andrée, he halted. She wanted to leave, but the other man would not let her.

—I was lucky enough to meet this Fräulein. The Fräulein is perfectly at home here, she must be a painter.

His friend lifted a pair of black, somewhat small eyes positioned very closely together.

—Stay, Fräulein. I'm also an ignoramus when it comes to art, so I'll take advantage of my friend's good fortune. The gallery will soon close. Do a good deed and acquaint us foreigners with your national treasures.

The trio walked around, chatting and laughing. The older man behaved as if he were an old friend of Andrée's. He said,

—My friend is an engineer, trained in America. He discovered a way to make cars stop traveling on the ground and instead fly in the air. Listen to my advice, Fräulein, don't travel in the machines that come out of his factory. I don't trust them. Who knows what my friend will think up next?

The closing bell started ringing so they went out to the street together. The foreigner suggested they go into a café, but Andrée declined.

—No, she can't, she needs to hurry home.

The Spaniards accompanied her to her house. The older one thanked her, regretted his vacation was ending. He was leaving the next day.

—But perhaps we will meet again someday.

The lively young man interrupted him.

—I will certainly see the Fräulein again. I'm leaving too, but later. . . .

His gaze took in her slim figure in her fitted, dark outfit and black hat. Her calmness and the respectability and appropriateness of her dress brought a pleased smile to his lips.

—Later—she said, stopping—later people forget. Adieu, *meine Herrn.*

The sadness that had hidden itself for the last few hours like a thief who waits behind the door, crept forth again. On the stairs, she bent down over the railing. The black-haired Spaniard was standing at the entryway writing something into his notebook. Hastily, she ran up to the fourth floor.

The next day Andrée came to her new workplace. The salon was not large. The few rooms made a homey impression: soft, low couches, soft divans, flowers, soft colors.

The factory was working on a large order for a revue in a small well-known theater. It was the first time the shop was working for a stage performance. Everyone in the workshop was in a good mood. Andrée threw herself into the work like a starving person going after food. Drew, combined contemporary and older fashions, designed. She worked zealously, making the interests of the firm her own. She enjoyed handling materials, cutting, creating.

In the reviews of the play's debut, the press underscored the originality of the actresses' clothes. Andrée had the satisfaction brought by the first bit of fame and threw herself into her work even more: rising early, going to bed late. From the workshop—home. The fear of the next day that had gnawed away at her since childhood disappeared. She felt her muscles expand and her energies grow.

In the winter, her employer gave her a gift: a fur collar, imitation blue fox. Andrée was delighted with the gift.

At about the same time, Andrée met the Jewish girl who had been let go from the workshop where both women had worked. The girl spoke French a bit better than before and said she was now employed making cardboard boxes. Things had improved for her family. Her mother was baking cookies and had a large clientele. But her father earned almost nothing. The Cossacks had broken his arm and he couldn't do much work.

Andrée told her to come to the salon. There was a lot of work and the owner agreed to take on the girl. On the first Saturday, a Jewish woman in a long dress and a large apron brought Andrée a gift of sweet cookies.

After the new year she received a postcard from the young Spaniard: his work in the provinces was finished. Would the Fräulein like to come to the museum on Sunday? He would wait for her.

They began to meet. Not too often. He traveled around for his firm and worked in the office even during holidays. But from the very first day, they met as good friends, mostly talking about their work. He was planning new improvements in the manufacture of automobiles. She was excited about colors, forms. All the while they observed one another.

That's how the damp, rainy Parisian winter went by. Buds began to appear on the trees, quickly filling with sap. From the sap emerged thin, spiky green stems. The sun cast down its hot, golden smiles. Slowly, shyly, the green stems opened, drew into themselves the sweet breath of spring, and overnight the hard, black branches were adorned with delicate little leaves.

Flowers were everywhere on the street, flowers on the boulevards, in the houses, flowers on the bosom of the girl running in down-at-heel shoes carrying a box with leather straps over her shoulders, flowers in the lapel of the newspaper boy with the loud voice, flowers everywhere—a city steeped in greenery and flowers.

People felt an elusive longing for spring: elderly people thought about what might have been and was not; the young waited for something that must come, looked around, were impatient. Agitated nights. Fantastic dreams tangled in sleepy heads. Heated bodies restless in their beds. It was blossoming time.

One Saturday evening, after a hot, muggy day, Andrée and the Spaniard sat near the smokestack of a small steamboat traveling on the Seine. The boat was returning to the city. On the opposite side of the smokestack a market woman was dozing with a basket of vegetables at her feet. Under his arm, a shriveled old man holding a package wrapped in stiff paper kept spitting into the water. From behind the smokestack a sailor appeared in a sweaty shirt and slowly went down to the engine room.

The sun had already hidden itself, but the air was still steeped in warm light. A blue-red veil swayed wearily in the river; from above, drops fell constantly onto the veil; mother-of-pearl colors, reddish-violet, clear blue, flowing corals. They spread out around the ship, chased one another, disappeared in the water and appeared again. Near the shore, under clumps of trees, behind fences, reeds were already casting shadows and a secretive darkness emanated.

The boat went along under the grand Parisian bridges. Andrée had seldom had the opportunity to be there, so the Spaniard called out the names of the bridges.

—One of the Louises built this extravagantly carved stone bridge. And that other one shimmering and burning with gold like a dressed-up nouveau-riche man, that's the Russian czar's bridge. Where are they now, those powerful rulers? Existed, did many things, built, destroyed. Gone. Millions of people had enjoyed themselves under these girders, looked through this mother-of-pearl veil, lived, disappeared. The two of them were alive now. For how long?

That thought brought them closer. Without intending to, they moved nearer to one another. She took off her hat. A breeze played with strands of her straight, dark hair. He saw the movement of her delicate girlish throat so close to him. A blue vein meandered down to her bosom and disappeared under her low-cut dress. His breath quickened. He touched the blue vein with his lips. She shuddered so much that he moved away, surprised. He bowed his head and looked at her intensely. Two large steely eyes blazed. Slowly he stroked her dark hair. She did not move.

At their station, they said goodbye.

—Be well, Andrée.

The simple, familiar words made her smile shyly. The steely eyes lit up again.

There are times when empty days creep like fat black flies in the autumn, and the clock on the wall yawns out long gray hours, slowly, one after the other, and again one after the other. If one recalls such past weeks and months, one thinks they really did not last that long: every day a year and from that year no memory remains, nothing to hold onto. At other times days fly by, hours chase one another, the week, the month, the year are full of events, experiences, as full as a big, powerful current and one cannot believe such a small amount of time could have encompassed so much.

Andrée's life now swam on such a powerful current. Until reaching this shore, she had lived fully, intensely, with the responsibilities of work. Now there was bright, warm joy in every hour, every minute. Love came to her so simply and familiarly that, often, she was barely conscious of it, like a person who pays no attention to the air she breathes. Love, which mostly brings disappointment and sorrow, smiled on her, warmed and nourished her hungry, languishing heart. Now the quiet, proud first hand would tilt her head, as she was wont to do, and suddenly laugh aloud over nothing. Every little thing made her feel childlike, profound joy. Happiness slowly smoothed over the thin crease at the left corner of her mouth, that thin strip from her lip downwards that came from the times when everyone, whether they needed something or not, ordered around the errand girl from

morning till night, hurrying her up and down the stairs so that her
feet ached so badly at night. Or perhaps that thin crease had appeared
during childhood, in those long winter evenings when the orphans,
like little hens, sat huddled together in the damp corridors of the old,
rotten building, quaking in fear and misery, and on the wall a small
lamp winked blindly, and the black, naked branches, threatening with
emaciated fingers, banged against the tall, dark windows. . . .

# V

One evening, Andrée did not come home. She returned late at night
and ran quickly past the caretaker's window.

Miguel now spent very little time in the office, mostly taking work
home. He sat near the window, drew, figured things out. Andrée would
come, take off her coat, put on an apron, dust the books strewn about,
straighten the pictures on the dresser, pour fresh water into the vases
holding flowers that she often brought. She went around quietly, like a
mouse, so as not to disturb Miguel. He always felt her presence, sensed
the charm she brought into his bachelor's room, often looked around,
smiled, and once again focused on the papers on his table. Sometimes she helped him with his work, drew something, copied his notes.
When he was most occupied with work, she went out, shopped, prepared something to eat on the gas cooker. But she always went home
in a timely manner. She never stayed as late as she had that first time.
Seldom, very seldom, did he come to her. Only by day, briefly, to pick
her up or just to stop by for a minute. She did not want people to see
him too often at her home. He agreed. It was better to be in his room.

Neither of them had much money. He worked in a factory and didn't
earn much; the improvements he had made in manufacturing were still
being tested. She didn't make much money either. The business was

doing well, but it had very little capital. Every month there were worries about how to cover the expenses, so her salary was small. And then there were the wardrobe expenses: the first had to wear fine, modern clothes. Andrée, who had always cared about clothes, now dressed very well and even became a bit coquettish. Living like this, one month followed another.

That winter, Miguel wanted to spend a few months in the south of France near the Spanish border. His parents had long wanted to see their son. Since coming back from America he had only been home once, for a short visit. They could meet near the seaside in the town to which his factory was sending him. He was often sent on trips, working at various branches of the firm. But this time Andrée was worried. She didn't even know why. She thought about his family, whose photographs she had seen. His father had been a major in the Spanish army. An old man of average height in a strange uniform. The son looked just like him: a small, reserved face with a pointy beard. His mother—a gray-wigged woman in an old-fashioned stiff collar and a few strands of small pearls on her ample bosom. Entirely unfamiliar people. He also had two sisters, one a teacher in a public school, the other a clerk in a municipal office, both of them old maids. Until then, Andrée and Miguel had always been alone, alone in the big city, not needing to pay attention to anyone else, no one caring what they did or how they were living.

Andrée thought Miguel must be having similar unsettling thoughts, but was, as usual, silent. Actually, neither of them were talkative, especially not about the past. But one time the Spaniard did talk about his lineage: they came from a very old family, were once rich, but had become poor a long time ago. His father was seriously injured in Morocco in a battle with a local group. He had a small pension and in the evenings he worked as a bookkeeper. They had a small house outside of town. He, Miguel, had always been drawn to mechanics. Because he had been involved in the workers' movement, he had to leave school and go to America where his parents had an acquaintance. His father was still serving in the army then. The Spaniard said little about his time abroad. What was there to talk about? Ran around with newspapers, carried a peddler's wares, was hired in a factory, went to lectures at the polytechnic institute in the evenings, worked hard, sometimes went hungry—just like every émigré.

Miguel left without even saying goodbye. He was very busy that day and telephoned from his office to the salon. That used to happen often: he would get orders from his boss, call up, say "Be well, Andrée," and leave. That's what happened this time too. Nor was Miguel big on writing letters. A postcard, one letter a week, and nothing more. Andrée was used to that. It was the way things were meant to be.

Something important happened in the salon: the arrival of a sales agent from South America who traveled to Paris twice a year to buy fashions from the first-class, world-renowned firms. She spent a few hours in their workshop looking at the dresses prepared for the summer season. The next day she came back and asked to have a considerable number of things packed up. This was a great triumph for the business. Such large orders could put the young business on its feet. The owner, who was spending a few weeks on the Riviera, was called back. She came quickly in order to complete and sign the contract with the agent. All energies were mobilized to make the customer happy and deliver the goods on time. Andrée threw herself into the task. For her, the work was more than a test to determine if she was capable of directing a large, fine salon. The work occupied all her thoughts, every free moment, leaving her no time to reflect. The first few boxes had already been sent to the agent, who was to take them back to South America. The absolute busiest time was over. It was clear the whole order would be filled on time, and the hardest work was done.

The Spaniard did not write for a long time. He had sent a postcard from a well-known winter resort. He was probably there with his family. Since then, no word. The old sense of dread, which had so often gnawed at the heart of the lonely girl, that old uneasiness crept quietly nearer, snuck in like a thief who stands silently at a locked door. Happiness had come and chased away the dread. But not for long. In fact, it had never been far away. It stood close by, waiting for happiness to die, for joy to burn out. Then, in the dark, her old friend, unhappiness, would slip back in. Andrée fought the unwelcome guest, refused to give in to it. Such is life, awful, dull life. So what? Didn't she have her work, the one friend in the world that never disappoints, never deceives?

Like all healthy, proud people, she did not deny the worth of what she had, did not blame anyone, did not disparage the flowers that had once bloomed for her. Miguel had not written—maybe he was ill? If so, his friend from the office would certainly have let her know. That is what they had always agreed on. And he wasn't alone: his parents and friends were with him. Even if he were ill, he still wouldn't need her.

One morning she stopped at the telephone, put her hand on the receiver, wanted to call. Stopped. Maybe he would never return to Paris? Go to a different branch of the firm? And if he did come back, maybe he no longer intended to see her? In the office, they would note that she had asked after him. She stepped away from the telephone. Did not call. Wrestled with herself. Overcame the awful longing. But that little crease on the left side of her lip made itself known again.

It was late at night. The workshop was almost empty. There were only a few workers who were completing a pressing order and Andrée stood bent over a large table with curved scissors in her hand. Someone rang. It was probably the agent who was supposed to see displays of new samples. The boy at the door said a gentleman had come and wanted to speak with her. Andrée put away the scissors, wiped her hands, and went out.

Miguel was standing at the door. They extended their hands to one another.

—I arrived today. I have to go to the office right away to prepare my report for tomorrow.

They sat on the narrow couch in the front room. He looked at her. Noticed how bad she looked.

—I didn't write. I couldn't. I promised my mother.

She was silent.

—Listen, Andrée, things with us have to change. Do you hear, Andrée?

She was silent. Her steel-grey eyes asked, but her heart already knew.

—The office told me about an apartment, not far from here. Go, take a look at it tomorrow.

—Tomorrow?

—Yes, my elderly parents are coming to the wedding.

—Now, in the middle of high season?

—I know, but my father can only be free a month from now, not later. My parents want to get to know you as soon as possible.

The month passed quickly.

They walked slowly on the wide boulevards. It was a sunny, mild day in the month of Tammuz. Miguel looked at his watch.

—We still have over an hour. Our appointment is at 12:30, and my parents won't be at City Hall before noon. We can continue walking.

In those hours, the tall trees barely moved. Andrée opened her coat and breathed in the lightly scented air.

—I want to tell you something, Andrée. I know it's meaningless to you, but you must hear it.

She looked at him calmly. Both were silent for a while.

—Do you remember, Andrée, that you once asked me about the Marranos in Spain and Portugal? You had read something about them.

I explained to you then that they are Jews who were forced to convert by the Inquisition. These Jews always sought marriage partners among themselves. That's what's done to this very day in many families. My father comes from Marranos and is a distant cousin of my mother's. One branch of my mother's family remained Jews, and still follow their old faith today. For hundreds of years they lived in Toledo. You know I am the youngest child and the only son. I was very sick when I was ten years old. No one expected me to live. My father was then garrisoned in Africa. My mother was frantic. She went to Toledo to her aged great-grandmother whom she had seen once in her youth. In the Toledo synagogue my mother vowed her only son would be a Jew if God granted him life. That's what happened.

Andrée stood still for a moment. Before her closed eyes swam the little framed painting that hung on the wall in her mother's home. In the painting, the sun was reflected off the snow, golden rays came in from the wide, low window and mixed with the yellow glow of tall copper candlesticks. A hazy light hovered around the men, wrapped in white. . . .

—What is it, Andrée? Why did you tremble?

—Me? Nothing. . . . Let's hurry, Miguel. Come. Your mother is waiting.

She took him by the hand.—Come!

A small group of people stood near a green, dusty table: the young couple, an elderly dignified man with a pointy beard and a few Spanish medals on his dark jacket, a large woman in a heavy silk dress and a pointed collar over her ample bosom, exactly as in the picture, the head of Miguel's office, Andrée's employer, a few friends. The official wearing the red badge of the French Legion of Honor on his chest looked at the bride,

—Who is your mother?

—A French woman, a Catholic, a laundry worker and then a model for artists, no longer alive.

—Your father?

—A painter from Poland. I do not know his name. I am called by my mother's name.

—Who are you?

—A worker, a seamstress, a Jew according to the wishes of the father I never knew.

There was a rustle of heavy silk, a stifled sigh. The marriage registration continued.

After the witnesses signed the certificate, the Spanish woman embraced her daughter-in-law, pressed her to her ample bosom, murmuring,

—Forgive me, my child, for not having wanted this match. I always dreamt my son would marry a Jewish girl. Forgive me!

Hot tears fell from the old eyes onto Andrée's inflamed face.

After the wedding everyone was invited to the young couple's apartment for a glass of wine. The factory's administration had given a sum of money in honor of the engineer's wedding and the two small rooms were properly furnished. A lovely vase with flowers stood on the table, a gift from Andrée's employer. Andrée sat next to her mother-in-law. The old woman held her hand.

—I am happy—she said—I am happy that Miguel's wife has no other relatives. She will belong entirely to us. . . .

Removing her strands of pearls, she put them on her daughter-in-law's neck.

—These pearls belonged to my ancestor, a woman who was burned at the stake in Toledo.

The director of the factory, a lively middle-aged Frenchman, clanged a knife against his glass. As was customary, he made the first speech. He was getting ready to announce his candidacy for the next parliamentary election in the area where the factory stood. He spoke about the difficult conditions in the country, the weak, incompetent government, the new parliament. Raising his glass, he ended by addressing the young couple:

—Long live the two representatives of the modern working class, the children of an old-new people who possess the treasure of endlessly new energies and the eternal strength of the young. Long live our only sovereign, work!

The Spanish woman bent down to the bride.

—You will come to visit us soon. We will travel to Toledo where, in the old synagogue, my son will marry his wife according to Jewish law.

The first delicate rays of the sun had barely begun to shine through the window when Andrée got up quietly, dressed, began to straighten out the apartment, wash and put away the dishes, and change the water in the flower vase still on the table. In the little kitchen, something was already cooking on the gas cooker. She ate, prepared Miguel's breakfast, and got ready to leave. Miguel woke up. Caught her at the door.

—So early today?

—I have to fit a few dresses on an old client who is going away tomorrow.

He embraced her and did not want to let her go. She freed herself, laughing. Tinkling silver bells resounded.

—Be well, my husband, be well!

And she ran quickly down the stairs.

# The Decree

The car clattered up the steep street, fell into holes of mangled pavement, scaled tall mounds of hardened snow, flung itself from side to side. Finally, it threw itself onto the wide boulevard and took deep breaths with its exhausted steel lungs. The chauffeur, a soldier wearing a short leather jacket, righted the car and no longer strained to turn the wheel or drive the swaying machine.

The street stretched out, straight, white, framed by two rows of palatial homes and villas built in various styles. Surrounding them were fine iron and bronze grates or elaborate gold-plated wooden fences through which could be seen old overgrown orchards. But the tall windows gaped—without panes, with broken frames. Here and there were pieces of glass, remnants of the expensive etched panes that had sparkled in the sun just a few years ago. During the cold, hungry winters the window frames had been used for heating, the windows broken and sold piece by piece in the marketplace. The empty houses stood in ruins. Their owners had fled, disappeared. Hardly any people could be seen on the street. The boulevard lay vast and empty. Only a few automobiles dragged themselves along the battered road, honking frightfully.

The chauffeur stopped at a two-story villa belonging to a well-known magnate, a high-ranking official. Shtoltsman jumped out of the car, opened the oak door with its carved coat of arms, ran up the marble steps, and went into a long room next to what had been a greenhouse once known for its rare, beautiful orchids—the owner's pride. Now a soup kitchen had been established there for the comrades employed by the local municipality.

The long dining room was teeming with tables full of people. Dozens of comrades sat in the middle of the room around a pair of long, narrow planks perched on top of two overturned boxes. A woman checking ration cards stood at the entrance near a torn, ornate armchair.

Shtoltsman looked around, searching. An elderly man stood up from a table on the side, gestured to him and called out—Here! With difficulty, Shtoltsman pushed his way through and greeted his comrade, who had once been chairman of the local legal council. Then he took off his warm leather jacket, tugged on his belt, and patted his gun, holstered with a leather strap. He sat down at the table, stretched his feet in their tall boots, shook the lock of hair on his forehead, and once again looked around. He was greeted politely and with respect from all sides. The young lawyer, Shtoltsman, had an important job, was considered capable and serious, a sharp, polished man straight as a ruler. He was held in high esteem.

—What would you like to eat?—he heard a girlish, quiet, melodic voice behind him ask.

—Today we received a sack of flour, so in addition to kasha we have latkes.

He turned around quickly, so quickly that his glasses fell off.

—Where did you come from? I've been looking for you for quite some time.

—Today I'm a server; I'll bring your food right away.

The young woman standing in front of the two men was short, sedate, holding a plate in the graceful, thin fingers she inherited from several generations of teachers who were far removed from any kind of physical labor. Her ancestors belonged to a rabbinic dynasty well known in the region. She looked at Shtoltsman with soft eyes.

—Latkes, right?

And she left. The young man wiped his cloudy glasses with a handkerchief.

—A strange girl—he thought, and felt, not for the first time, disappointed.

His comrade, the older lawyer, said,

—A typical small-town girl, a respectable one.

Shtoltsman raised his head.

—You know her?

—I even knew her deceased mother. My dear treasure, I mean the wife I treasured, lies on the road to their shtetl. I know the whole family. Recently, a Jew from there came to me saying the shtetl asked the rabbi to leave for his own safety. It's not yet quiet in their region, gangs are still roaming around. But the old rabbi didn't want to abandon his Hasidim. He did, though, send his orphaned granddaughter, Leah, here to the big city.

For a while the men were silent until the lawyer pushed away his plate, wiped his moustache with a piece of gray paper, and continued.

—The girl quickly got used to her new conditions. She is already working in the administrative office. Even though she's not pretty, she is one hundred percent full of womanly charm.

Shtoltsman kept quiet, obviously not wanting to continue the conversation. His older comrade looked at his pensive face and smiled into the woolen, tattered shawl around his neck.

A tall young woman entered, greeted Shtoltsman, holding his hand for a moment.

—Why haven't we seen you lately?

Without waiting for an answer, she walked on. A different server brought Shtoltsman's food. Making her way between the tables, Leah did not come near him again. A commander, a tall, handsome youth, suddenly grabbed her hand. Two large pistols glimmered on his belt. He wanted to take the plate from her. The girl would not give it to him, laughed a bit, caressed him with her soft eyes, turned around, and walked away. Shtoltsman stood up, put on his jacket, and said goodbye to the man sitting next to him at the table. He walked slowly through the room. Leah was standing near the wall slicing bread on an expensive table that was coated with bronze but was now broken, resting on two boxes. The slices looked like pieces of brown limestone. He stopped to say,

—I'll wait for you downstairs. Come soon.

Without lifting her head, the girl answered,

—I'll come right away.

Outside, Shtoltsman paced back and forth on the sidewalk. A cold wind blew from the river. It bent the naked trees beyond the fence, piercing his skin with sharp, icy needles. Shtoltsman's disappointment grew. Why was she letting him wait in the cold? And why hadn't she come to his table? Was she simply making fun of him? And then there were the absurd conditions that such a small-town girl put on him. It was truly a farce!

He pulled his sheepskin hat lower over his forehead, paced, and thought further. After all, what did he see in her, and why was the old lawyer babbling about her exceptional womanly charm and respectability? That man was just as much an unregenerate bourgeois as the girl's grandfather, the eighty-year-old rabbi somewhere far away. They were all the same. And, really, Leah was no better. Prettier women wouldn't reject him. For example, the educated, proud Comrade Ivanova often looked wistfully deep into his eyes. How strongly she had pressed his hand today, not at all wanting to let go. He would stop eating in the dining room and forget about the Hasidic privileged girl. He wanted to leave immediately and regretted having sent his chauffeur away.

Behind him, quick, light steps approach. He turns to see her small frame coming closer, wrapped in her short coat. He takes her arm.

—Come, Leahle, we'll go somewhere to drink a glass of tea.

—I don't have time. The old man filled a whole table with papers.

I have to type them, will undoubtedly have to work again until seven o'clock this evening.

—I'll take you to the law offices right away.

—Really? That would be good, she says happily and snuggles closer to him.

They start going down to the city. Lower down the wind was not so sharp and breathing was easier. The sun set over the frozen river. The large red ball dropped and was mirrored in the hard ice.

Near her office they remain standing at the balcony, behind the gates. He takes off his gloves and pats her frozen cheeks.

—My velvet girl.

He presses her to himself, falls on her half-opened lips. She disappears into his arms, becoming one with him.

Breathlessly, they tear themselves away from one another. Shtoltsman straightens up, is silent for a while.

—In the coming days I am traveling to the provinces. The meeting will take a few weeks.

—Really? where are you going this time?

He names several towns.

—You're going past my home, she says quietly.

He puts both his hands on her shoulders.

—Come with me, Leahle! If you really want to, we'll register. You'll be my wife. Good?

She is silent. Lowers her head.

—You're silent, Leah? Don't you know I can't do otherwise?—he says, impatiently.—Don't be a child, Leah. You must understand that my convictions won't allow me to go to a rabbi with you. You know that very well. You're playing with me. It's pointless. You don't love me.

—If I didn't love you, I wouldn't kiss you.

She straightens up. The hint of desire in her eyes is extinguished.

—So what? You still say you want to obey your grandfather, you don't want it any other way.

Footsteps are heard descending the stairs. The girl raises her head. Beneath her fur hat, two lines, like black snakes, appear over her thin eyebrows. She looks sharply at him.

—I can't do otherwise.

—Then you should know. . . . But she has already entered the building.

Irritated, he puts his hands into his jacket pockets and quickly walks away.

# II

Shtoltsman was very busy before his departure: meetings until late at night, working in the office, preparing materials for his trip. He also had to write the final paragraphs of the new decree so he could give it to the delegation before leaving. So he took himself in hand, thrust the little girl with her laughable bourgeois demands out of his head.

The next day when, before dinner, the chauffeur asked,—To the dining room?—Shtoltsman realized he had not thought about Leah all day.

—Home!—he said, smiling contentedly.—I'm fed up with moldy groats and stale latkes. It's enough!

His landlady would prepare food for him. He smoked a pipe, looked at the smoke rising in the frosty air, and kept smiling. A girl's silly notion! She promised the rabbi, her grandfather, that she would not get married without a wedding canopy. It really was a joke. What did he, a committed communist, have to do with a rabbi's grandchild, an orphan who had spent her whole life in the benighted, fanatical environment of a Hasidic enclave! In Odessa he had seen Hasidim who used to come to his father, the doctor, to be treated. His father was also in the Party. What a match! They would have laughed at him!

Completely calm and smiling now, he stretched out in the car, closed his eyes, and took a nap.

Shtoltsman came home late in the evening. As usual, he sat down at his desk, looked through his papers, skimmed the note with the telephone numbers of those who had called. He shrugged his shoulders; Leah's name was not among them, nor did she call the next day.

Shtoltsman went home early the next day. He wanted to write a few pressing letters and rest before his trip. But he had a headache. He lay down on the sofa, closed his eyes, was unable to sleep. His temples were hammering. Suddenly he remembered how Leah had put her cool hands on his forehead. He had a headache then too. That evening he had kissed her for the first time. Since then, they met often. He knows he loves her. And she? That day, on the frosty street, she had leaned into him, hidden herself in his arms. Such warmth came from her! Her skin always breathed hotly, burned. What made her so proud? Look at how offended she was because he didn't believe she loved him! All of a sudden she had become so angry. Her fiery cheeks turned pale and her voice was cold and strange.

Shtoltsman tossed and turned on his bed, unable to sleep, thinking: such a foolish girl. She didn't even want to look at him. She simply walked away. She was insulted over nothing. Such a privileged person. Turned her head and walked out as if she didn't even know him.

Shtoltsman slept badly that night. His headache was gone by morning, but he was still uneasy. He got up but could not focus on anything, paced the room with long steps, looked at the clock, made a telephone call, and went out.

In the front room the landlady stopped him.

—What's this? Going out into such a frost without tea? My cookies are ready!

The landlady, who had once been rich, trembled over her tenant, knowing that only because Shtoltsman lived in her house was she able to keep her possessions, which she had with great difficulty kept from being requisitioned. Sometimes he also did her a favor. Because of his connections, she was able to get a pair of shoes. In addition, her tenant paid for everything, so she took very good care of him, and saw to it that he had everything he needed.

But that morning Shtoltsman left without tea.

# III

The government-appointed rabbi, a Doctor of Philosophy and a poet, had just fallen asleep. He had sat until late at night near the little tin oven, writing, blinding himself by the light of the improvised lamp, and tending to the makeshift wick in his jar of oil. He was writing his memoirs. During the day he kept his notebook in the kitchen hidden behind the rusty faucet because he feared someone might find his notes. He would only write in his diary late at night, describing what had happened during his unsettling days. He wanted to leave a memoir for his sons in case he never saw them again.

His wife had gone to bed earlier and asked him to take pity on his weak eyes and go to sleep.

He joked,—Pity on my eyes? Maybe you mean pity on the expensive eyeglasses?

He has barely gotten warm under the fleece covers when he hears something under his window and springs up. The neighing of horses, a knock on the door, the too familiar knock of a rifle at the entrance that was barred with wooden boards. Leaning on his elbows, he listens. He glances over at the other bed where his wife is sleeping, snoring loudly. He lies back down, waiting. From a distance, he hears the barricaded door open. He hears loud steps going up the stairs and angry ringing at his door. Startled, he puts his trembling feet into his warm slippers. His arms have trouble finding their way into the warm robe.

—Sara, get up!

But she is already up, lighting the jar of oil and shivering from cold and fear. Their maid comes in.

—It's an inspection.

The three of them shuffle toward the door.

—Who's there?—stammers the rabbi.

—Open up. We mean you.

The rabbi's fingers flitter aimlessly. He is unable to turn the key. An impatient fist bangs on the door.

—Open!

His wife pushes him aside, undoes the chain, opens the door. The sparkling bayonets of two rifles appear. A man in a long, hooded fur cape enters. Wearing a large fur hat, he looks unnaturally tall in the flickering lamplight. A little being stands next to him, wrapped entirely in fur.

The rabbi does not move. He looks at the tall man and cannot utter a word. What could they be searching for in his house? Has he hidden the diary well enough? His heart grows cold and heavy. The lamp shakes in his hand. His wife takes the jar of oil from him. They go into his office.

—Comrade rabbi—says the man in the cape—we've come for you to marry us.

The rabbi sits down on a chair near his desk. His voice returns. Quietly, he says,

—Do you have papers?

The man takes off his fur hat, undoes his cape. At the belt of his short leather jacket two revolvers stick out of their holsters. He hands over some papers.

The rabbi nearly faints when he reads the name of the bridegroom. He takes off his glasses, wipes the lenses, looks the bridegroom in the face. Yes, it really is he: it's Shtoltsman. He recognizes the small face with the lock of hair on his forehead. He saw his picture in the newspaper. Recently he read a report about the speech Shtoltsman gave concerning the new laws governing citizens' rights: religious wedding canopies—he said—were now forbidden. Registering was only a temporary transition in response to administrative and political needs. It was only done in order to placate the backward population still steeped in its bourgeois mentality.

With trembling fingers, the rabbi turns to the second paper: Leah Svirski from Gostinietz. What? Maybe she was the Gostinietze Rebbe's grandchild? He raises his head. A short, graceful girl peels herself out of the yellow fur, a pair of soft, embarrassed eyes peering out of her narrow face. Nimble hands unwrap the woolen kerchief covering her dark hair. The bridegroom calls out, rather impatiently,

—The wedding canopy must be put up immediately because we're going away before dawn. The sleigh is waiting downstairs.

—The canopy? Now, at night, the office is closed and I have no scribe.

—This must be done immediately, Comrade Rabbi. I'll call for your scribe right away.

The two soldiers at the door lift their rifles, ready to go. A girlish, melodious voice interrupts.

—Comrade Rabbi, we're going to my grandfather in Gostinietz.

The old Doctor of Philosophy straightens his shoulders, smiles into his gray beard, thinking to himself,—What a match for the Gostinietz Hasidic court!

A few more jars of oil are lit. The rabbi puts on his black jacket. The samovar is readied. The soldiers bring in the scribe. Without having looked at the note sent by the rabbi, the Jew comes in half alive. A minyan of Jews is gathered from the neighboring apartments. The bride sits on a couch with her head leaning on the bridegroom's shoulder, nestled in his arms. She is napping, her delicate lips half open. She breathes loudly and comfortably, like a tired child. Shtoltsman covers her with his cape.

The minyan gathers. A bit of wine is found somewhere. The rabbi makes a blessing. At the threshold of the office, his wife appears.

—Mazel tov! She offers them tea and a plate of cookies, baked with dark rye.

The couple says goodbye. The rabbi touches the girl's dark hair.

—Send my regards to the Rebbe, my child.

A blue curtain hangs from the sky, dispersing the black shadows of night. The boulevard's frozen trees are etched on the dawn's whiteness.

The sleigh arrives. Flanking the coachman, the soldiers' rifles gleam. Shtoltsman's tall fur hat looks gray. Dawn is breaking.

The rabbi, smiling, cheerful, stands near the window. He looks at the departing sleigh. Tomorrow he will have lots to write in his notebook. And since he is a Jewish Russian intellectual and, as he calls himself, a *vosmey dyesyatnik*, an "'80s man" who romanticizes the 1880s, and because he is a poet, a lyricist, his soul sings a song of soft, girlish eyes, love, the dawn that dispels the shadows of night, and of decrees.

# Director Vulman

## I

The engineer, Marcus Vulman, director of the largest sugar factory in the region, returned one evening after spending several days in the city. On the occasion of his return, he invited a few of his longtime employees to eat supper in his "palace"—that's what people called his large house with its massive columns, where rich landowners lived before they squandered their wealth and sold the property on which new owners built a sugar factory and opened a stock company. The top floor was always closed and the large, richly furnished salons were only opened when stock brokers gathered for their yearly meeting. The director lived on the first floor. A gorgeous path of old, lush lindens led to his apartment, and right next to his windows lay a sprawling lawn full of flowerbeds.

Five men were gathered in the vast dining room waiting for the director and talking about the news he had brought from the city. When Vice Director Duval, a Swiss engineer, went to meet the director at the train, Vulman told him that all the city's administrators had been replaced. There was a new leader there. Nonetheless, it was thought the sugar factory would be left alone because of the importance of sugar production for the entire area's economy.

The director came in, cheerful and refreshed after his bath, elegantly dressed in a light, white, summer suit.

They all sat down at the table, drank in honor of the director's return, and began a lively conversation. Vulman told them what was happening in the city: a whole pack of new people were there. They were young, almost boys, and they had taken over the positions of the fired officials. Storm troopers were marching in the city, forcing Jews off the streets, singing terrifying militaristic and antisemitic songs. There were stories about the arrest of prominent men, social democrats and known pacifists. Among them, of course, were many Jews. There was no doubt the new rulers would go after the factory's personnel on political grounds, but according to the director they would not dare touch the administrators. The beet farm had so enriched the workers it would be idiocy to destroy the economic foundation into which so much money and energy had been poured.

The director's coworker, the Swiss Duval, a Calvinist and a social democrat, spoke up.

—Their entire system is without any sort of ideology, without a single new thought. In order to throw the tortured, depressed Germans a bone, they thought up this Aryanism. It's an excuse made up to oust their competitors—the Jews—without trouble and without any kind of effort.

Zaltsberg, the chemist who had returned from Berlin two weeks earlier, remarked,

—And in order to establish a dictatorship, they instituted a coordinated system of totalitarian rule. That's how they won over big industry and the Prussian landed nobility, which had been losing sleep for fear of the socialist proletariat.

He spoke calmly, but like a young boy, and his eyes were bluish and cold, like ice in the sun.

Vulman straightened his broad shoulders.

—Here, far from the center of things, we know almost nothing, but don't worry, the common sense and decency of the German people will soon free them from this dreadful rape.

When the group began to go their separate ways, the director kept the chemist back.

—Stay a while, Zaltsberg, let's drink another glass of beer!

They had a long conversation. Vulman liked to talk and was not indifferent to the impression his words made on people. The chemist was a well-educated, capable young man and, as the director had learned in the city, he was much lauded in social democratic circles. It was pleasant for Vulman to see how attentively Zaltsberg listened to him and how interested he was in the conversation.

It was quite late when Vulman accompanied his guest out. Standing on the terrace the director—excited by his own words—said in a voice ringing through the surrounding stillness,

—When you've been with this longer you'll understand that here, on this land, people need only one thing: work. Work and knowledge. Don't think the common man, the worker, doesn't understand that. His instinct and his work on the land tells him this. Give them schools, ever more schools, and opportunities to work and the *folk* will know what to do with the rest. The key to a better tomorrow lies in knowledge and work. Man has convinced himself that he rules the world, but what do we actually know of the treasures abounding in nature? Nature for us is still as it was tens of thousands of years ago: a sealed book whose first pages we have barely begun to turn. You and I concern ourselves with chemistry, which has the power to free people from the gnawing worry over their daily existence.

The chemist stood on the terrace steps, his face lit by the sliver of a new moon. Vulman gazed at the young man's pale, chiseled features and saw how a fleeting cloud cast a shadow over them, making his countenance seem strange and frozen in pain.

—Good night, Zaltsberg.

—Good night, Herr Director.

# II

The next day, earlier than usual, Vulman went on his daily inspection of the factory and the large property for which he had been responsible for the last ten years, and toward which he had always shown intense interest and great love. On the estate, in the granaries, around the workers' living quarters—everywhere the exemplary order he had instituted reigned.

The morning was bright, cloudless—a sign the recent troubles would not last.

Kuntz, the old German overseer who had worked in the factory for a very long time, stood at an open barn through which a baling machine had just been taken. When he saw the director, he approached him quickly, smiling, jingling the large bunch of keys at his belt. They walked on together.

—What's new, Kuntz? All's well?

—All's well, Herr Director, but Wilhelm, the foreman, disappeared suddenly, gone without a word.

The overseer stole a glance at the director. It was very hot and the sun was blinding. Walking past the factory building, Vulman stepped away from the footpath to stand in the shade of the wall that seemed cool and damp compared to the fully exposed path.

—So what? Did you pay him?

The overseer smiled under his long mustache, discolored by wind and sun.

—Was that drunkard owed anything? Disappeared and that's all.

But the director had moved on to other things. Hastily, he left the overseer and went home. The tree-lined path was cooler. The leaves on the old lindens swayed gently, thin sunbeams stole through them, and, like long golden mosquitoes, pricked his throat and greedily drew the sweat from his heated face.

The green grass of the meadow, whose flowers seemed like a colorful carpet, spread out in front of the window. Vulman thought about the city's turbulent but deadening, stifling life. He looked around, and, as was his habit, he patted his thick gray hair. With all his being, he took in the surrounding beauty and calm and the joy of being at home again. Spryly, he went up the steps to the terrace.

Duval, the Swiss engineer, stood up from the rocking chair. Both men were hungry and began eating breakfast.

There was a knock on the door. Zaltsberg came in.

—Drink a glass of coffee with us, Vulman called out. The chemist took the glass from Duval and sat down at the table. Without raising his head, he said,

—Wilhelm, the foreman, hasn't returned. . . .

—I know. Kuntz told me. Why are you suddenly interested in the foreman?—the director asked impatiently.

—Peasants have come from the village. Yesterday, they saw Wilhelm in Warburg with a rifle on his shoulder. Three people were shot there yesterday, among them two Jews who refused to leave their shops.

All were silent for a while.

—So it means they're after us—Vulman said, standing up from the table and throwing down his crumpled napkin.

—Gentlemen, let's go to the office.

After the director and the bookkeeper looked over the day's accounts, Vulman ordered the cashier who paid the day laborers their wages to go immediately to the nearest farm and settle accounts with its overseer; en route, he should stop at the miller's and settle the overdue accounts there as well.

The cashier took along a large sum of money and drove his light truck past the office window. As usual, he was carrying the keys to the iron safe. Vulman called to him through the window.

—Drive straight through the woods, and don't stop for anything!

The cashier answered,—That's just what I was planning to do—and turned into a side road.

On the director's desk lay many letters and papers. The bookkeeper entered the office several times. A merchant came from town. The overseer of a small farm belonging to a shareholder's organization sat in the office for a long time. The work proceeded calmly and smoothly, like a well-oiled wheel. Everything went according to plans the director had established at the beginning of spring, and all the reins were in the director's hands. Absorbed in his work, Vulman forgot about what was happening in town.

It was not stuffy in the office. The overgrown birch tree in front of the window kept the heat out. The sunny month of Tammuz breathed into the room with the fragrant scent of the orchard, the warm fertile earth. A light breeze whispered. Everything spoke of life and creation.

Voices and hoofbeats were heard near the gate. No one in the office moved, as footsteps pounded on the porch. Vulman went into the office with two uniformed men—one a typical Prussian in an elegant uniform and high riding boots and the other a short, fat man with a slight hunchback and a surprisingly shrill voice. His small, sharp eyes were hidden behind dark glasses.

A young boy was leading two saddled horses back and forth near the window. Wilhelm, the foreman, sat on a wagon.

The man in charge looked around, took a large pack of papers out of his briefcase, and read out several names.

—Director Marcus Vulman, the bookkeeper Shtern, the chemist David Zaltsberg, the manager Schultz, and his son Kurt, a student in a technical school.

Kurt Schultz, who had recently graduated from a vocational high school, was not in the office. The manager, standing on the porch, was asked to bring the young man. Meanwhile, the man in charge paced around the room and impatiently tapped his riding crop against his boots. The student entered.

—Is everyone here? Hand over the keys to the safe and the warehouses. Surrender your weapons!

No one had any guns or knives. The bookkeeper explained that the keys to the safe were with the cashier, who had gone to a farm a little while ago.

—Really—said the man in charge—never mind, we'll find a way around that!

He looked around the office.

—In the meantime, come here please.

Through the window, the detainees saw Duval approach the man in charge on the porch and say something to him. The man dismissed him with a wave of his hand.

—Leave me alone! All Jews are communists and the student, Karl Schultz, was well known at school as a revolutionary. Don't bother me, just be glad you're not on my list. Get out of here!

It was quiet in the office. The bookkeeper, Shtern, sat on the plush sofa barely conscious. The chemist stared out the window. The director stood leaning against a bookcase, remembering that he was supposed to have gone to a nearby farm. Yesterday, he had brought books and other things from the city and promised to deliver them today. Helena was waiting for the things she had requested. He saw before his eyes her white face and red lips—lips Helena would often moisten with her tongue—and he felt her pampered body near him. The last love, he thought, reflecting on his relationship with the wife of the owner of a farm near his family's summer home.

They had corresponded, met one another in Berlin in the winter, spent hours in hotels and private rooms in restaurants. During summers, there were frequent—very frequent—visits to the farm where her husband, a high ranking official, spent no more than a few weeks. Lately their daughter had become sulky. She probably understood. . . .

Almost immediately, Vulman forgot about the other men near him. He just stood there, thinking of nothing at all.

The other officer—the short one—came in. His sharp, pointy blue eyes took in the men. Smiling, he said,—Please, gentlemen, come outside.—And suddenly his grimacing face erupted in anger.—March!

They were stood against a wall, in the shade, amid nettles made dry and gray by the heat and dust. It was exactly where the director had stood that morning. Vulman leaned against the damp, cold wall and glanced over at Kurt. On the dark, sunburned face of the student a pair of insect-like, large black eyes sparkled. Their eyes met, but Vulman lowered his head, not answering Kurt's silent question. Zaltsman, the chemist, stood stiffly upright and his face was once again strange and frozen as it had been yesterday evening on the moonlit porch.

Shtern's wife and Mrs. Schultz and her two daughters appeared on the lawn. They tried to stop the strangers, grabbed the hands of the passing officers, begged to talk to their husbands and father. The men standing at the wall heard their distraught voices.

A few soldiers in ill-fitting uniforms and crumpled hats sat down on the footpath opposite the men, guarding them and gnawing on cucumbers. In the distance, the overseer could be seen running toward them. The ends of his linen coat were blowing, and he was showing something he held in his hand. But no one understood what it was about.

Director Vulman thought about his family, about his wife, whom he had married while a university student in a provincial city. He had been living not far from the university in a room in a small house owned by a doctor who worked on a merchant ship. The doctor was away for much of the year, attending to the sailors. At home, in that little house, the orphaned niece he had raised kept house. The doctor was close to retirement when he suddenly became ill and, within just a few days, died on board the ship.

Returning home from an outing with other students one night, Vulman was clattering around on wobbly feet. As he went up to his room, he heard loud sobbing. Feeling his way, he turned around and went to the door from which a light shone. In the small room, there were walls covered with pipes and pictures of ships, tables full of seashells, and large vases on the windowsills. The doctor's niece lay on the sofa with her head buried in an embroidered pillow, sobbing bitterly. On a table, the student found a telegram from the office of the Hamburg Shipping Company telling of the tragedy. He sat down near the girl, pulled her hands away from her weepy, rather unattractive face and tried to calm her. But the girl shook her head and did not stop crying and bemoaning her loneliness and the fact that she had no alternative now but to go live among strangers.

—Don't cry. I'm here. I've been living with you for two years now. Don't cry. I won't leave you alone. I'll take you to my parents.

The girl could not be comforted because her dead uncle had been like a father to her. Vulman bent down to her.

—Listen, if you want to, we'll get married, but don't cry. Calm yourself.

The next day he could barely remember how he had covered the crying girl with a warm blanket and gone upstairs to his room. But without waiting to be brought his coffee, as he was accustomed to do, he went down to the old doctor's apartment and the very same morning he repeated his proposal.

Vulman had a large family, at the head of which was his father, a provincial lawyer with a successful practice. They were displeased to learn of his unexpected marriage. But Vulman himself never regretted having bound himself to the old doctor's niece. She quickly adjusted to her new circumstances and since she was a practical, goodhearted woman she became the one everyone in the family went to for advice.

Whether sitting at the bedside of her ill father-in-law or bringing some order to the neglected household in which they spent their summers—everywhere the doctor's quiet, unattractive niece stayed on the sidelines, a stranger in the cheerful, boisterous family.

Standing now at the cold, damp wall, Director Vulman, for the very first time, asked himself whether his wife had been happy in his home. Did she love him, or had she just gotten used to the frequent romances which he had never wanted to or tried to conceal?

A strange weariness now took hold of Vulman. A shiver went through his spine, and the burning rays of the sun glistened in his eyes. People appeared on the footpath. The leader with the pointy eyes approached, raised his hand and shrieked,—Get out of here!—At first, Vulman did not understand. He stepped away from the wall, took a few steps, noticed that Shtern had torn himself away from the wall, and saw Schultz's pale face.

A shot rang through the air. Vulman turned around, saw Zaltsberg bend forward with outstretched hands.—Oh—Oh—Oh—Oh— could be heard coming from the chemist's open mouth.

Then another shot and an unearthly cry that drowned out all other sounds was heard from Schultz, Kurt's father. Like a drunkard, the warehouse manager banged his head against the old birch tree, wrapped his arms around its thick white trunk, and fell silent.

The director and Shtern, the bookkeeper, were led away into the office.

—Take out the money. Open the safe!

—We don't know how. . . .

The overseer entered. He was so agitated he could barely speak. He announced that he had long since sent for the cashier, who would certainly come soon.

—We don't have time to wait. Hand over what you have!

Behind the office stood workers with a few carts from a nearby village cooperative. They had come for sugar and were not allowed to leave. Relying on the director's voucher, they surrendered the money they had brought with them. The factory staff collected it all and brought whatever anyone had.

The man in charge took the money, some horses, and a wagonload of sugar, and they all left.

Wilhelm, the erstwhile foreman, sat on the cart that took them away. As he passed the office windows he hurried the horses, shouting,—Depend on it, we'll be back!

Duval, the Swiss, excitedly took the director's arm, staring into his eyes.—We came out of that well, dear friend.

A hot wave coursed through Vulman's heart. The movement of his legs seemed a miracle as once again they became limber and his steps certain. Happiness flooded his breast: he again recognized the aroma of the quietly growing flowers, again heard the rustle of leaves on the old fir trees, again took in the magical evening orchard, and understood the warmth in Duval's friendly touch on his arm. Aha! Once again alive. Among the living. Alive again.

The teary, fat cook stood in the dining room along with the grinning boy who served the food when Vulman's wife was not there. Vulman saw the set table and wanted to eat. Greedily, he went at it, eating everything the cook quickly prepared. He smoked a cigar and went to his room, threw off his shoes, stretched out on the bed and fell asleep the moment his head touched the pillow, not waking until morning.

# III

A telegram was sent to Zaltsberg's mother. It came back with a note saying Frau Zaltsberg was on vacation in the mountains. It was not known where.

Jews came from the village. The chief of police sent a telegram saying that the men who had been shot should be buried as quickly as possible. The dead were still lying in the office.

Someone came from the nearby farm with a message. They knew what had happened in the sugar factory. Helena wrote that she and her daughter were getting ready to leave for town and she asked Vulman to go with them. They would stop for him at the factory on their way to the train.

The director reread the note several times. He went over to the table to write a reply but thought better of it. He stood deep in thought for a while, called the man who had brought the note, and told him he couldn't travel today, but he would come to the train to see the women.

Near the building where the factory's personnel lived, it was very quiet. A young gentile nursemaid was wheeling the cashier's baby back and forth in a carriage, and Schultz's two little girls were running to the ice cellar to get ice for their mother, who had a bad headache. In the distance, their thin braids could be seen bobbing up and down on their backs.

In the afternoon, Vulman lay down to sleep. In the evening, the overseer came. He urged the director to get away and stay in the city for a while, until the situation became clearer. Duval also tried to convince Vulman not to stay on the property any longer.

Suddenly, Vulman realized it was almost too late for him to get to the train. Maybe he should ride over? He got up, wanted to call for a horse to be saddled quickly. In his thoughts, he saw Helena, a quiet, elegant woman, saw her lips red as cherries, and near her, her daughter, the student. Well, we'll see one another tomorrow in town, he thought indifferently. He sat down once again on the sofa near the window, was very tired, and once again he could taste the sweet, dull taste that had been in his mouth yesterday, after the shooting at the factory wall.

That night, he fell asleep quickly but jumped up suddenly, as though someone had jabbed him.—Oh—Oh—Oh—Oh—he heard coming from a frightened, faltering voice. He turned on the bedside lamp, sat up, spit out the nauseating saliva in his mouth, sat for a long time on the edge of the bed, lay down again, and again fell quickly asleep.

In the morning a telegram arrived from Helena: she was uneasy, she begged him to come as quickly as possible.

Funerals for Zaltsberg and Schultz's son were held on the same day. The two wagons carrying the dead came from town at almost the exact same time. The Jewish cemetery was nearer, so the chemist was buried first.

Vulman walked next to the wagon. He had not known the chemist well. Everyone was hurrying to the second funeral. The managers and workers had known and loved the happy, young student since his childhood. They were all devastated and overcome with sadness and compassion over Schultz's tragedy.

Very few Jews from the area were at the cemetery when Zaltsberg was buried. The small group of hired hands and workers quickly dispersed. The director, with Shtern and the overseer, drove to the church. There, too, the funeral was done quickly. Vulman left his car for Schultz's family and took a two-wheeled cart home. He ate hardly anything at lunch and, lost in thought, he said not a word. The Swiss looked at him thoughtfully for a while.

—What's wrong with you, Herr Director? Have you lost your healthy appetite?

Vulman lifted his head, looked at the Swiss.

—Have I lost my appetite you ask? Yes, I can't anymore.— Grimacing, he pushed his plate away.—Yes, I've lost my appetite, lost it completely, he repeated, as though Duval's question had clarified for him what he had merely dreamt until then, and only now did he understand what he had been thinking.

•

Before going to sleep, the director, as usual, went outside to walk in the garden and smoke a cigar. It was not a bright night. The sky was covered in grey clouds. A fog rose from the lawn slowly covering the walls of the factory, and it looked as though the roof and the chimneys of the building were swaying on tall, foamy waters. Vulman's body melded into the surrounding fog, and the glow of his lit cigar could be seen wandering back and forth on the footpath. His thoughts wandered with it, seeking and not finding an outlet.—Tens of thousands of years have passed and not a single thing has changed. The cruel, dreadful soul that lived in people when humanity just barely emerged from the Stone Age, that same cruel soul lives in the modern gentleman, he who conquered the earth and the air. Sweating and struggling, man constantly builds new treasures only to destroy them in blind fury, driven by hunger and thirst, seeking a bit of joy, and once again destroying, trampling everything underfoot, just as they had trampled and thrust into rotten nettles the body of the happy young man with the sparkling black eyes who had looked at the world with such curiosity. And the other one?—Once again Vulman remembered how the chemist had stood before him on the porch, his intelligent, clear eyes mirroring his thoughts, and again he saw his helpless outstretched hands there, near the wall. . . .

Vulman walked more quickly, the fog around and within him growing thicker.—So, it means that a person goes and further and further before him goes his mind? His proud mind? It's a lie—the thin riding crop cut through the heavy, stifling air—a lie. It goes not before him, but after him. The mind runs after a person. Slavishly he obeys the orders of his ruler, murmurs to him, polishes his lowly instincts with fine words. And the higher a person climbs up on stilts he built for himself, the lower he falls and, frightened by his own audacity, quaking because of the heights he has reached, he sinks into the dust and dirt.

Vulman was almost running in the darkness and with a muted shriek his whip cut through the gray fog.

—What's next?

A sudden weariness engulfed the lonely man. He threw down his cigar. Its red glow swayed in the air and fell somewhere in the darkness.

Director Vulman sat on a bench under a tree with his hands pressed between his knees. He thought: But he is a Jew! Jews are brave. Yes, that's what they are. But he? Is he truly a Jew? His grandfather, the doctor, his father, he himself, what connection did they all have to Jews, to those very different Jews there on the other side of the border? He felt like a German, loved Germany with all his soul, was proud of the country he thought of as his, the land of high culture and infinite possibilities. He had always lived happily and contentedly here. Faults? Everything isn't yet as it should be? Yes, he knew that, but Germany seemed to him like a large building that was being erected. The foundation and the walls were done, and very soon the scaffolding would be removed, the dirt swept away, and the sun would shine through tall, gleaming windows. Holding onto this idea he, Vulman, could enjoy his life, travel the world, love women, and work. Work.

The factory? The thought made him tremble. The factory into which he had put all his powers, the factory which was his creation.

Vulman sat for a long time bent over, barely able to straighten up.— And so, what of it? If they don't demolish the factory, even if they take away the property of the shareholders, some ninety percent of whom are Jews, Duval, the honest, devoted Swiss would still be able to figure out how to run things.

Now Vulman thought about his wife. She would lack for nothing. After all, several years ago he had transferred ownership of their house in town to her. A warmth engulfed his heart—his wife, his wronged wife. . . . Maybe things would be calmer for her, maybe she would finally be free of the stress and tension he had always caused?

But not for a second did his thoughts go to the woman whom he thought of as his last love. . . .

The crescent moon appeared behind the old linden tree, bowed over the tree and, like an impatient partner, looked into the darkness where Director Vulman sat, tired, not thinking, with a strange emptiness in his entire being.

Suddenly he stood up. Enough. He started walking toward the house. The fog crept after him, hiding his way back. But Vulman did not look around. Cheerfully and lightly, as always, he quickly went up to the porch, closed the entry door behind him, laid his riding crop near the mirror, and went into his room.

The lamp was lit on the night table near his bed. Director Vulman pulled open a drawer, took out the small revolver he always carried when he rode around the property. The electric light flickered on the weapon's glossy steel.

A shot tore through the house.

When Duval ran into the bedroom, he first noticed the untouched bed. On the couch near the open window lay Director Vulman. His strong feet were dragging helplessly on the floor. A faint rasping from his mouth could be heard.

Lights were turned on in the quiet rooms. People came running.

At dawn, without regaining consciousness, Director Marcus Vulman died.

# Who?

large, poorly lit room. Over the table, a lamp with a wide, brownish yellow lampshade descends from the ceiling. The hazy light flits around the tablecloth, gilds the metal sugar bowl, and splits against the facets of the crystal vase. Deep shadows have spread along the walls and corners.

The voices of several people mingle with the hum of a large samovar. They drink tea, listening to the buzz that is about to die out. One man, with a broad, stubborn forehead, sips from a glass and lights a cigarette. Another bends over the match and also lights his cigarette. Through the fringes of the lampshade a narrow ray of light cloaks the bowed head. A dark beard hangs momentarily above the table and dips once again into the thin, brownish blackness. The one to the left of him stretches out his hand, picks up the match, and lights his burnt-out cigarette, puffs on it, looks at the thin circles of smoke rolling above his head, smiles, and says,

—During the war no one would have dared light three cigarettes with the same match. It would have seemed like an omen that, at the first battle with the enemy, the third smoker would undoubtedly be shot. . . . It's not surprising that the World War nourished superstitions. When danger hangs over everyone and blind fate reigns, one grasps at anything, seeking logic in the unruly forces of nature, and believing in nonexistent powers.

—Superstition—the one with the broad forehead repeats, interrupting him.—Where are the borders between superstition and what we only believe is superstition? Perhaps we are mistaken because our minds don't understand, are not yet able to understand. . . . When our regiment stood face to face with the enemy. . . .

He stops, drags on his cigarette, slowly lets out a long, milk-gray puff of smoke.

—Something happened in our regiment.

He spoke of what he himself lived through and what others witnessed.

# II

Our positions were on a field covered with a dense pine forest. Some small, young trees were strewn about on the lush grass. They looked like children who had mischievously run away from their mothers. The serious old fir trees, standing like a wall, took care of the youngsters and guarded the forest. It was evening. Blue shadows embraced the strong, deeply rooted tree trunks, but the tops of the trees were enflamed by a setting blood red sun that seemed to ignite the forest.

One of the soldiers, a baker's apprentice from a small shtetl, stands at his post with half-closed eyes blinded by the hot blaze, listening to the weak sounds of shooting coming from a distance. He is chewing grain kernels and thinking about the package that arrived from his shtetl that morning. It has been such a long time since he has taken a bite of a roll, and the couple of shirts would also certainly come in handy. It's bad enough that he has been wandering around the front for eight months. He has not seen his wife in almost a year.

He smiles, remembering how his Rivka would sit in the small room at his mother-in-law's, holding the baby at her breast, the house smelling of freshly baked warm bread. He would go there during Sukkos, when he expected to have leave. At this thought, he shifts to spread his crooked feet even further apart, the feet bent from standing whole nights over the kneading trough, and the pleasant memory makes him shut his eyes tighter.

Suddenly, from behind him, the commander of their unit appears. His head leaning to one side, as it usually does, he peers out from under his thick, black eyebrows, bends his narrow back, and lightly shuffles his feet, clad in tall, well-made boots, barely touching the moss near the trees. The soldier stands at attention, fixing his gaze on the commandant's face. Without stopping, the officer quietly issues a command and strides off.

—Leave your post.

The baker's apprentice sees him approach another soldier, so he takes his rifle off his shoulder. He does not like the order. After all, he is a soldier who has been given a stripe on his sleeve because he once found the enemy's position. But still, he is hungry and tired. He spits and mutters under his breath,—Once again, for a change, retreating, damn them!—And he swallows the curse with a handful of seeds he thrusts angrily into his mouth.

Evening falls. A quiet melancholy lies on the woods. A breeze caresses the small trees, bending and twisting the thin branches, dreamily sharing secrets with them. The soldier looks around, afraid of the secretive stillness, puts his rifle on his shoulder, and leaves.

There is a quiet panic on the post. The enemy is entirely still. No one could have expected such a retreat. In fact, they were getting ready for supper. The smells of cooking come from the trenches. Soldiers are carrying water. Then the field kitchen's fires are quickly extinguished and, still hungry, they retreat.

The next day they learn that the enemy had immediately taken over the abandoned position. From the division's headquarters comes the question: Why had the regiment left its post? Who gave the order?

There is a commotion in the regiment. The soldiers who had been standing guard say it was the commanding officer of their unit. The colonel sends for him.

Headquarters have been set up in an abandoned school. Clerks sit around a table in a large room. Cavalry and infantry men come in and out. On one side, near a window, the colonel listens to the commander's explanations: There was a misunderstanding. Yesterday afternoon he had been playing cards with some comrades. He names them: the adjutant, the enlistee, the clerk were all there.

The colonel puts two fingers in his collar, turning his head as though his collar is too tight. He doesn't like the young commander, can't stand how he always tilts his head to one side as though eavesdropping, unable to look anyone in the eye. He knows the man is a good officer, brave, always at the head of his company. Nonetheless, the older veteran colonel avoids him. So he doesn't respond, shrugs his broad shoulders, and leaves the headquarters.

# III

Not far from the front lay the estate of a landowner, well known in the region. At the beginning of the war a small hospital was set up on one side of the large yard, in a wing of the house that had an attic and a balcony. The head nurse, an elderly widow, has been working there for over a year. The landowner's son, an officer, was wounded and captured in Prussia, near the Masurian lakes. He is still sitting in a prisoner-of-war camp and it has been a long time since his parents have had any news of him. Their one young daughter, just out of school, is a devoted nurse and cares for the wounded in the hospital. There, she met the company commander when he would come to check on his men. They became engaged. Her mother doesn't like the match: she knows nothing about the officer's family, thinks he is a damaged man. Her father shrugs—in such times, one can't be too choosy. After all, the fiancé is an officer, just like their imprisoned son.

The girl is busy in the hospital ward when she is told that her fiancé has come riding. She is just about to end her night shift. She speaks to the head nurse, goes up to her room in the large house, changes clothes, and goes out to the veranda.

Seeing her fiancé, she smiles at him with bright, joyful eyes. The officer stands up from his chair, bends his head even more to one side, kisses her little hand, and takes in her supple shape. Under her dress, he can feel the strength of her young, sunburnt body, steeped in fresh air.

There is an earnest mood on the veranda. The old landowner is sitting silently near the table, a pipe in his mouth, blowing rings of smoke. The girl sits down, looks around, and asks quietly,—What's new? Are things bad again?

—No news—answers the officer.—There are skirmishes at the front. We're preparing for a big battle.

The girl turns her head, catches her fiancé's fiery glance, loses herself in it, lowers her eyes.

After supper the young couple go down to the garden. They walk on the long, straight path past old poplars leading to the lakeshore, sit down in the dilapidated gazebo on the hill from which they can see a meandering stream. Beyond the forest, on the other side of the shore, a full red moon rises. It hangs over the water, casts down silver ribbons that roll, stretch, struggle in the water. Beneath the hill, tall poplars lower their long branches, gaze longingly into the black water, and shudder quietly.

The officer embraces his fiancée, caresses her throat with his hot breath, burns her lips with his kiss.

—My dearest, I feel the bullet will not miss me this time. I see death standing at my side!—He presses her closer and whispers in her ear,—Love me, my dear, love me!

In the bedroom of the girl's parents, morning grayness steals through the closed shutters. Her mother turns in her wide bed, raises her head from the pillow, listens: the sound of horse's hooves can be heard in the yard. The old woman springs up, glances at her husband, at his large hairy hand hanging down helplessly, sees the ring that can no longer be removed from his thick finger, hears light steps in her daughter's room, and understands that her fiancé has just left. So late, she sighs, lies back down, closes her sleepy eyes, mutters, So late. . . .

On the balcony, the old noblewoman is watering the plants when she sees her daughter leave the house. The girl seems happier, lighter. There is a slight blush on her face, like that of a ripe fruit ready to fall from the tree. Her steps seem nimbler, her clear brown eyes glow.

—You came home quite late yesterday, and he left before dawn—her mother says quietly. Her daughter stands still, says nothing, looks at the two rows of tall trees reflected in the lake, at the golden rays playing there. She answers softly, pleading,

—Don't be angry, Mama, they're getting ready for battle. He feels death at his side. And I love him, Mama.

She goes down the steps. The sun pouring over her wraps itself around her and she becomes one with the surrounding light as she disappears behind the trees. All that can be seen is her tulle shawl snaking among the trees, fluttering like a pair of white wings.

The next evening, her fiancé arrives unexpectedly. Thick humidity hangs over the garden. Lightning splits the sky. From somewhere far away thunder comes rolling, rumbling. Every now and then the trees shudder, stand once again without moving, listen, wait for something. . . .

Both women are sitting on the veranda, sewing linens for the wounded soldiers, when the officer appears. They did not hear him coming. The girl is surprised, stays in her seat, lets the thick material fall onto her knees, blushes as her eyes sparkle. The guest refuses the offer of tea, does not sit down, says he is in a hurry and must leave soon. A little while later he asks his fiancée to take a walk with him. He has something to tell her.

The young couple have barely left when the mother goes to her husband. The old man is engrossed in his newspaper, examining the map he has spread out on the table, and moving around the little flags showing the front and the army's new positions. His wife stands near the table.

—He's here again—she says, and glances at the map. The man looks up at his wife, smiling good-naturedly.

—You've forgotten, old lady, that you too were once young—and again he bends down to the newspaper.

The kind nurse, returning from bathing in the lake, climbs the hill and sees the young couple below her. She wants to go to them and, as she comes nearer, she hears the officer's hoarse voice coming from behind the bushes:

—Yes . . . it was a mistake . . . I can't forget the other one. I love. . . .

The nurse stops, understands they have not noticed her. Through the low branches she sees the girl stretching out her arms to her fiancé, murmuring something with white lips, imploring him with deadened eyes. The nurse tiptoes away, down the hill. Before she enters the footpath, she turns around without really intending to. The girl is sitting bowed down, with her face in her hands. Over her, leaning to one side, stands the commander. The nurse thinks he is whispering something into the girl's ear. Lightning splits the sky and huge drops of rain soak the earth. The nurse has had a headache all day. She is cold and goes home. Lying in her bed, she sees the man walk past her window and leave the garden. Almost immediately, she is called to come to the main house because the young lady has fainted.

Standing near her daughter's sofa, her mother tells the nurse that when the girl came in from the garden she went to her room saying she would come down soon. Hearing something fall, her parents had run upstairs and found their daughter lying on the floor.

The nurse takes the girl's hand, looks into her pale face.

—It's nothing. See, she's already opening her eyes.

The girl's father approaches with furrowed brows.

The girl soon comes to herself. She smiles a bit, says she had suddenly felt lightheaded. Now she feels fine. She drinks a glass of tea, takes off her clothes, and lies down in bed. She wants only to sleep. Nothing more, just sleep.

The nurse stays with the worried parents for a while, calms them, says she saw the young couple in the garden, hadn't meant to listen to them, but overheard a few words.—They must have quarreled. That often happens between couples.—The mother sighs. Before leaving, the nurse and the mother go upstairs again and find the girl asleep.

That night there is a storm, but in the morning the sun is once again shining. The mother goes quietly up to her daughter. The room is empty. She waits, wonders, searches the house, inquires at the hospital. The old shepherd, who has served the family since the landowner's grandfather lived on the estate, comes and says that at dawn, just when he led the sheep to pasture, he saw the young lady on the other side of the shore. She was walking among the trees. It was very cold.

The old shepherd struggles to get the words out. Barefoot, he stands on his thin, brown feet, leaning on his tall, knotty staff and looking like a dry, chopped tree trunk with two roots. He leaves. People are sent to look for her in the forest, at the riverbank, in the fields. The drowned girl is found that afternoon, her white tulle shawl knotted in her tangled hair.

Her fiancé is sent for. He comes right away. Clutching his head, he denies he was there yesterday. He has no idea what happened. He has witnesses to prove he was with his friends in the trenches all day and then spent the evening with the colonel.

After the girl's funeral, the regiment decides that the unit commander should resign his commission. He leaves and is never heard from again.

Thus ends the story told by the man with the broad, stubborn forehead. It grows quiet around the table under the low-hanging, brownish yellow lampshade. Behind the men, long shadows creep out of the corners.

A woman in a white apron enters, sees the lamp is dim, goes over to the wall, turns the electric knob. It grows bright and cozy in the large room.

# An Incident

This morning, control of the city once again changed hands. One set of occupiers retreated, another took over, but it didn't make much of an impression. People were used to such changes. In a few days the steel helmets would surely return.

He lay in bed listening as the infantry marched in. He was tired, so he closed his eyes, remembering the girl who left him late last night. The girl—how had that happened?

At the beginning of the world war, he had set out for home, rushing to the border. But he had to stop and wait for transports and permits. Then foreign powers came and took control of the city. He could not move from there. He got a room in an empty apartment the owners abandoned when they fled further inland. An elderly maid was taking care of it. He knew no one there, but he had to stay and wait.

Once, pacing his room, he saw the girl. Standing on tiptoe in the window of a haberdashery, she was busy arranging a display, hanging up merchandise, her hands grimy, her bosom thrust forward. An energetic, healthy girl. He had seen her a few times in the courtyard where her parents, the shopkeepers, lived next to their store. He had spent the past eight long years among strangers, wandering, without real work, without real interests. Around him were other émigrés who, like him, lived for news from home. Some days, they would meet and pretend they were accomplishing something, drawing up resolutions that achieved nothing, drudging along, superfluous, unemployed people among the surrounding population. They waited, not knowing for what. They lived their bitter émigré lives and, just when the war finally gave them a chance to return home, he got stuck, alone, a foreigner.

Seeing the girl in the haberdashery window that day, he stared without really intending to. His blue eyes darkened, looked hungrily at her body, greedily took in her lively, happy face. The girl was embarrassed and jumped away from the window.

Smiling, he recalls how they met in the soup kitchen, grew closer. A good girl, a kind, innocent girl. She brought joy into his life. Since his student days, there has barely been any time to give a thought to the fact that he was still young. He was always drowning in work, always feeling as though he were being chased, always afraid. He sat in prison several times. It was the girl who reminded him that he was still a young man. He gets warm all over when he thinks of the girl, of how she caresses him, never asks questions, surrenders her young body to him, trusts him, does not even know his real name, and understands him.

The morning sun pours into his room. He turns toward the wall and falls into a deep sleep.

There is a piercing, impatient ringing in the entryway. Heavy footsteps of soldiers in the house. The foreigner opens his eyes, tosses his blond hair, listens. An officer comes in, stands at the threshold, looking around. The man in the bed recognizes him.

—Ah, how quickly that dog shed his skin. He's already wearing a different uniform.

It's an unfortunate coincidence, but "that dog" recognizes him too, has certainly not forgotten how many times the man in the bed had made fun of him, how the man had rescued his comrade from the officer's hands.

—Ah, the provocateur.

The man grabs his revolver from under the pillow and, without even raising his head, shoots the officer twice.

He misses. The bullets hit the wall near the door. The officer jumps back, quickly closes the door behind him, calls for the men guarding the gate downstairs. Soldiers come running. A loud order. Soldiers with drawn guns tear open the door and enter the room.

The bed is empty. They search every corner of the room, tap on the walls, look in the bathroom, the kitchen, everywhere, but the foreigner has disappeared. The officer telephones to raise the alarm. Soldiers surround the house and the neighboring houses on both sides of the street. Guards are placed at every entrance and no one can enter or leave. A high-ranking officer comes to investigate. Everyone who lives in the courtyard is questioned. Suspects are arrested, most of them young men.

The girl is frightened and does not know what to think. She goes around half dead, but after a few days have passed and the foreigner—the bold shooter—has not been found she begins to calm down. The young man must have saved himself and run away. She cries bitterly, longing for him, but keeps repeating his words to herself. When she once asked him what would become of her when he left, his blue eyes had lit up. "I need you, my dear girl. We will never part. Do you believe me?"

The man is not found. The houses are closely guarded.

Five days later, at around six in the morning, the janitor is carrying a garbage barrel out into the courtyard. He stands still when he sees someone in white summer pants and a nightshirt, his bare feet in summer shoes. The man is holding onto the wall with both hands, moving slowly, looking everywhere. His tousled blond hair covers his forehead. He is shuffling along like a blind man, looking like a thin white shadow.

The janitor recognizes him. It is the vanished foreigner, the one who shot at the officer. The janitor quietly puts away the barrel, runs to the watchman at the gate and says, "He's here. The shooter has been found."

The soldiers run into the courtyard, grab the unfortunate man and ask him where he has been. The foreigner answers quietly, "A drink of water, bread, give me a bit of bread. I can't bear this anymore." The man is hardly able to stand on his own two feet. He is trembling from exhaustion and hunger.

"Where were you?" the soldiers ask, looking around.

The foreigner points. "There, in the cupboard under the stairs."

It is a very narrow cupboard belonging to an empty, poor apartment.

Neighbors come running. The authorities are called, and the courtyard fills with soldiers.—There, in that cupboard?—No one can understand how a person, even one who is neither big nor tall, could last in that low, narrow cupboard.

"Water, a drink of water." The foreigner can barely move his lips. Someone gives him water and another thrusts a piece of bread into his hand.

The girl hears the commotion in the courtyard, runs out of the house, sees him, and wants to run to the wall where the foreigner is standing, but her father holds her back. "Father, let me go," she says, trying to tear herself away.

The officer appears. "Take him!"

The foreigner throws down the cup of water and jumps to the side. His blue eyes grow dark, cutting into the officer's face like two sharp daggers, and he is pale with anger and hatred. The soldiers draw closer, with outstretched hands. The foreigner twists and turns with unnatural speed, jumping like a trained acrobat. He is a whirlwind. A hoarse voice calls out,—Bayonets!—The foreigner straightens, hangs for a moment like a white shadow in the air, and falls. . . .

An unearthly cry shakes the courtyard. The girl drops to the ground, fainting. She is taken to prison, held for a long time, questioned day and night. No, she really knows nothing. She does not even know the foreigner's real name or what town he came from. She knows only that he is an émigré. Nothing more. She is sent back to her parents.

•

Late at night. It is quiet on the bridge spanning the lake. Few passersby, now and then a car, a droshky, or a wagon coming back late.

A woman stands leaning against the railing, looking at the dark, steely stream. Onto the shimmering mirror of water, electric lights from the opposite shore cast bluish specks like bits of a fire about to burn out. The specks look like lanterns shining beneath the water. They attract the eye, show the way.

The woman at the railing unbuttons her coat, moves closer, thinks for a while about her mother and father, shakes her head. That one, the foreigner, was the one she loved more than anyone in the world. Why hadn't she sensed his presence, sought him out, crawled on her hands and knees in the courtyard, on the steps, searched in every corner? He had waited for her, perhaps called to her. She might have been able to save him, bring him food, hide him at night. Oh, how he twisted there, threw himself around like a hunted animal in the forest surrounded by dogs and hunters. No, with that image, day and night seeing that image, it is impossible to live. It would be better, much better, to drown in the stream, here, where it is deepest and the bluish fire sways like a lantern.

She looks around the bridge. No one is there. She grabs onto the railing, bends over—one minute and she will be in the lake. Suddenly she feels a thump, something moving inside her body. She clings to the railing. It would be better. . . . But she cannot move from the spot and stays hanging onto the railing. Again, a movement, a thump inside her. She understands—oh, oh my, the baby's first movements. His baby. She straightens up, leans against a pole on the bridge, catches her breath and runs as quickly as she can to the middle of the bridge. Far, as far away from the lake as possible. She goes down from the bridge, drags herself home, murmurs with dry lips,—I would have drowned his child. His child!

•

Months go by. The girl gives birth and boards the child with someone just outside of town. Every Saturday she goes to check on the little boy she is protecting like the apple of her eye.

Years go by, circling, spinning, running. Gradually, the girl grows calm. Marries. When her parents die, she brings the child back to live with her. What about her husband? They work together in the store, lead a respectable life. She is, as always, a quiet woman, her dark hair now sprinkled with a bit of gray. Her customers are drawn to her calm, steady demeanor.

When the store grows and they need a larger location, the woman will under no circumstances agree to move to another house. She will live here, only here. So they renovate, make their apartment into the store, and move to the upper floor. There, where the girl had found her destiny.

# Colleague Sheyndele

—Right. It's enough for today.

She is pleased, smiles, puts away her pen, puts the written pages in the desk, and stands up. Straightening her back, she takes a few steps around the room. She worked well today, succinctly and clearly explaining the results of the research she has been conducting since summer. The recent experiments have proved her hypotheses. She feels her work is a success. Now she will give a lecture at the Doctor's Association. The date has already been set. Then, if her findings are approved, she will submit them to a medical journal. She sways a bit on tiptoe. She is a little apprehensive. She has never published anything before. This is her first major work. She braids her fingers together behind her head. Bacteria are such an interesting world, so enticing. Once you enter it, it pulls you in further and further. She is glad she specializes in this field. She likes her work.

She remains standing at the window. The weather is nice. Her small apartment is in a spacious, bright courtyard. The snow is spread out like a large white carpet. What time is it? She lifts her hand to look at her watch: one-thirty. Today is her day off. She was in the laboratory in the morning and she has nothing more to do. Her one free day of the week. . . . Her son has gone on an excursion with his school. He will not be back for a while. She remembers how worried and upset he was that he might be late. He had to be wrangled into putting on warm socks and taking something to eat. All he wanted was chocolate and an apple. They dashed around the apartment, joking and laughing. Mottye was a well-behaved child, capable, good, all grown up.

She looks around: a very nice room with a bookcase and a few prints on the wall that are not at all bad. Behind the low screen is a couch, covered with pillows and throws. That is where she sleeps. At night, she hears her child breathing in the other room. All this—the whole household, the books, the instruments necessary for her work—all this she procured with her own energy and her own labor. She can be happy, things are good.

She shudders, remembering the awful days now well behind her. First of all, her marriage to the student. Her mother, Rachel, was a midwife and supported them for a few years. Sheyndele already had a child by the time her husband finished his degree and went to Germany to complete his studies. Then the war broke out. They were separated from one another until the occupation. And then . . . it was clear from the first answer to her letters that her husband did not want to and would not come home! Another woman had bound him to herself. Dazed, she had been with her child and her mother in the middle of her life. Where to go?

But it was not for nothing that Sheyndele was considered a good swimmer. Even as a young girl, she had been able to ford every stream. She used the little support her uncle sent from Africa to enroll in the university. She worked hard at school, spent summers working too. She used to come home briefly for the holidays. Finished. Finally surfaced. For the past two years she has been busy in the hospital, working in a private laboratory, making a living, and being with her son.

Sheyndele looks thoughtfully out of the window. In a year, she might be able to travel abroad to complete her training and learn new methods. She wants to advance, research, write. But for that she has to work hard and save money, devote herself fully to work. She stretches her none-too-big, none-too-full body. Determined, she shakes her short, brown hair. She really is working hard and saving money.

The sun is dancing on her clean, shiny floor. She wants to get out of town, to fresh air. It's too bad she didn't arrange to meet anyone. She feels empty today. Alright, she will go by herself.

But she doesn't move. She bends over the pale tulip on the table, touches its lush petals, breathes in the flower's hot, fragrant scent.

She listens. The phone is ringing.

—Hello, who is it? You . . . good morning. Yes, free. I was getting ready to go for a walk. Where? No, no. On foot, just outside town. Come to me? Not necessary. I don't have patience to wait. Where are you calling from? From the factory? That's not far from the road, is it? I'm on my way there. We'll meet. What? Soon, soon.

A quick look in the mirror behind the screen. She fixes her hair, opens her compact case: back and forth and done. She puts on her short fur jacket and hat. Calling to Leah, her son's wet nurse who has been with the child for many years, first at her mother's home in the shtetl and now with her, Sheyndele says, "Give Mottye warm milk when he comes home, and make sure his feet aren't wet."

The street is bright and noisy. People jostle one another on the wide sidewalks. Sheyndele hurries.

The hospital's old doctor and his assistant are sitting in the tram. The doctor winks at her. "Here, Colleague Sheyndele, over here." He has known her for a long time. Her mother, the midwife, used to send him patients from the shtetl. He always calls her by her first name. She pushes her way through to the two men. The assistant with the long, sad nose politely takes off his hat. He gives her his seat and holds on to the hanging leather strap. A year ago, he once accompanied her home from the hospital and told her that perhaps, in time, he might marry her because, in his opinion, they were a good match. Sheyndele had gotten herself out of the conversation and, as was her way, she had laughed a bit. The young doctor had pouted and looked down his sad nose. Today, however, Colleague Sheyndele is in a good mood: she is laughing and talking and joking with the men so that even the assistant smiles begrudgingly.

At her station, she parts from them with "Adieu, adieu!" and waves.

Soon she is on the road. She sees him in the distance. Here he comes, the American engineer. He was sent from a New York firm to set up machines for a factory in town. He lives in the neighborhood, has friends nearby. He felt at home quite quickly. They met one another on an outing in the summer. In early winter, they saw one another at the ice rink where she sometimes went to pick up Mottye. "The technician," as he is called, showed the boy all sorts of tricks on the ice. He accompanied them home and since then he would visit them from time to time. She went to the theater with him occasionally. Now they are taking a walk. His steps resound loudly on the frozen ground. He moves quickly and lightly. The fresh air carries them both along. They feel no urge to talk. It is still light, but a wide, reddish curtain with violet borders descends over the woods. It lights up the old fir trees that, from a distance, look like a zigzagging wall.

"How is your son?"

She answers. They are again silent. Pleasant breezes waft around them, rocking and intoxicating them. Slowly, scattered snowflakes fall. On the reddish curtain, a few stars sparkle and shine with all the colors of the rainbow.

There is a field on the right. In the middle of it stands a lonely old apple tree. Its broad, low-hanging branches are covered with a fine lace veil. Sheyndele points. "Let's go there." He takes her arm and they seek out the narrow, barely trodden path.

It is very quiet under the tree. The snow can be heard falling off the branches. Evening descends from somewhere up above and surrounds them. Sheyndele stands leaning against the tree and looks thoughtfully into the distance. Blue shadows hover over the field. Blue evening shadows weave a magical net around two people under the old apple tree on the white field.

Suddenly, hot lips touch her face. For a moment, they burn like fire on her cold skin.

Taken aback, she raises her head. Motionless, face to face, two pairs of eyes measure each other. How long? A moment? A lifetime? Facing his keen, hungry look, she lowers her head. In the dreamlike quiet, there is only their hot breath.

Then she shudders, tears through the white lace veil, rips the magical blue net, runs out of the field. The evening has covered their tracks. She runs and her feet sink into the deep snow. She cannot go any further. He runs after her, lifts her up and carries her over the field. In order not to fall, she throws her arms around his neck and presses her face against her frozen fur collar. A cold shiver makes her tremble.

When they reach the paved road, he puts her down. She opens her mouth, wants to say something, motions with her hand, is silent. Her hat has fallen to one side. She is very pale in the evening light.

Sadness overwhelms him, a quiet sadness grounded in passion and suffering. Gently, almost ashamedly, he takes her arm.

"Come, let's listen to what the blue evening will tell us. Come, sweet Sheyndele."

Behind them, the light snow covers their steps. In front of them, the lights of the town swim in yellow fog. From above, the young crescent moon bends down to the ground, curious.

# Our Courtyard

## I

My desk stands to the left of the window. Opposite me as I work, I see the long, two-story building in the courtyard, a building with no ornamentation, balcony, or attic to interrupt its gray, naked walls. In a few places, the bricks have crumbled. Two low doors leading to the ascending stairs look like dark holes.

Toward the left, not far from my window, a low-ceilinged wooden house stretches along the narrow courtyard. The janitor lives there, and near him lives a Jew with an atrophied, paralyzed leg. The Jew lives with his daughter, a pretty, cheerful, not particularly young girl. Toward the right can be found a warehouse and Khatsye the coachman's stable. That is actually the quietest corner of the courtyard. But on market days, at dawn, a familiar peasant arrives with a wagon of wood and the housewives come out of their dark, low-hanging doors. They stand around the wagon, chat about the inflated cost of wood and start bargaining. The peasant is silent and hangs a sack of oats on his horse's neck. Sometimes the women talk things over with the janitor. It is true he is not always steady on his feet, but Yan is, after all, their goy. They have all been living together in this courtyard for many years. It seems as if the wide felt hat he wears is the same one he has been wearing since before the war. But Yan was younger then and the felt hat that has grown green and mushroomy had then covered thick brown hair and not his current thin gray wisps. Well, no one gets younger and, anyway, hasn't he lived through a lot since then? After three years in the war, when he finally dragged himself from the rotting, wormy trenches, he came home to an unpleasant surprise. Yan takes a drink a little too often, but still, he's an honest goy. No one can say otherwise.

It's cool in my apartment. It's still early and the sun is not yet shining too brightly into my room.

An old linden tree is growing opposite me on a hill behind the wall. Its top bows over the roof. I love that tree. As early as the month of Nissan its many buds tell me the rich, fragrant summer will soon arrive. And here it is, the summer, and here, winking to me from the roof, are sweet flowers swaying on the festively dressed branches.

And soon, very soon, summer passes and the withered leaves cling with all their might to the naked, black branches, swaying and shivering in deathly fear. The cold wind rustles and bends the strong tree. It grumbles, seethes, and laughs brazenly. "Yes, the end of summer. The end."

# II

—Fayvke, Fayvke.—The sleepy quiet of a hot summer day is interrupted by a loud shriek.—Fayvke!—vibrates in the air. From the window opposite mine a red head of hair appears over a flaming red face. Fayvke's mother, a peddler, has left this red boy to watch over the wares airing on chairs. Old woolen and silk blouses, coarse cotton dresses wave near the window through which can be seen, in the middle of the room, various things strewn about and, hanging by a string from a lamp, a pair of small shoes with elevated heels. They sway coquettishly back and forth and turn their pointy, polished toe caps, as if asking, "How did we get here?"

—Fayvke!—yells the redhead loudly. Fayvke does not answer right away.

A Jew in a vest appears at a window to the right.—Stop screaming, you crazy boy. Look, look—says the man, and turns around to call to someone in the room.—Devorah's son Yoshke is about to fall out of the window, just look!

But the red-haired boy bursts out laughing. He bends even further over the windowsill.

# III

Yan, the janitor, comes to hang up my shelves. He enters the room, makes a show of taking off his hat and puts it on again slowly. He looks at the shelves and goes over to the wall. He's a bit drunk and when that happens, he likes to talk.

His girl, twelve-year-old Manke, brings in some nails. She curtseys and remains standing near the door, but Yan chases her away. He raises his hand and yells at her to get out: "*Pretch.*" The girl flees.

I know Yan loves that quick, dark-haired girl. I often see them sitting on the bench in front of their door. The child fills his pipe. He sends her to bring tobacco from the store, especially when it comes to getting it on credit. Sometimes Yan pats her on the head and they both sing a sad tune. But as soon as he has a few drinks—he doesn't need much—he starts to go after her. Then I know Manke will be beaten. I shake my head and say, "*Panie* Yanie. Hitting a child?" He looks at me weepily and two big tears run down his wrinkled face.

"Don't worry, *Pani*, I know they call me a drunkard, and that's the truth, I really have become an old drunk. But did I ever drink before, except on a holiday? I crawled on my knees for miles and miles with my wounded leg, hungered like a wild beast, hid in the forest from the Germans who chased us on the Riga road. I had only one thought—to get home to my wife and child. And once I finally managed to come home, what did I find? You don't know, *Pani*, how hard it was for me not to aim my rifle at that stranger, the enemy who robbed me even worse than the Germans did. God kept me from that sin."

Yan crosses himself, weepy and shaking. I interrupt him.

"Don't talk anymore, *Panie* Yanie, you mustn't speak about such things. Go and lie down for a while. You can hang the shelves later."

He wipes his face with his sleeve, takes off his hat, and leaves with drooping shoulders.

I know Yan's story. When the Germans beat the Russian army near Riga, he wandered for a long time with a badly wounded leg until he managed to get home. One morning, a peasant brought him to our courtyard. Leaning on his rifle, Yan went to his apartment and opened the door. In his seat sat a black-haired man. Yan's wife, Yulke, was half asleep in bed, her blond braids strewn on the pillow, rocking a cradle in which lay a small child. Yan's only son, already a big boy, lay, as always, on a straw sack in the corner.

Instinctively, the soldier raised his weapon. It was a miracle that Khatsye the coachman was just then leaving the stable, recognized the janitor, ran over to him, and grabbed his arm.

It worked out. . . . Yulke hid in the coachman's house. The dark-haired guy ran off. Once again, Yan swept the street, just as he had done before the war. Yulke did washing for the neighbors. The courtyard pretended not to know anything about the whole story, but the janitor began to drink more often. At the beginning, he would get drunk, beat his wife, and even hit the little girl. Ever since Yan started to drink heavily, Yulke has had to do most of the work. She has grown thin, with dark eyes. Her husband seems rather afraid of her.

The storm blew over. Life in Yan the janitor's home took on a routine. That's life.

# IV

Early morning. A thin, warm rain is falling. Patches of green grass appear near the wall facing mine. Flowerpots are put outdoors to catch the rain. Through the thin, crooked drops, the little yellow flowers on the linden tree shine like small flames. I sit at my open window and mend socks. The maid cleans my room. She has been with us in this house for a long time and knows all the neighbors and their families. Ours is a Jewish building. Many of the families who live here were once quite well-to-do. Were. But now everyone is impoverished: new conditions, high taxes, old debts. Auction notices hang on nearly all the stores in the neighborhood.

Our maid, the elderly Paulina, sweeps the house. With broom in hand, she stops near me and shakes her head. "Brand new socks and already torn." We both look at the holes in the thin material. "What a nuisance socks are these days."

From outdoors a soft wind pours in steeped in dew, earthy smells, and fragrant wet grass. It feels like honey pouring into one's lungs. One wants to be somewhere in the fields, on plush meadows near the river.

I ask Paulina if she can tell the red-haired boy not to scream so frightfully. He is bothering me as I work. Even in this heat, I often have to close my windows. Paulina dusts, straightens up a bit, stays seated on the sofa with the broom in her hand, and now—not for the first time—I have to listen to a story about the neighbors.

Before the war Yoshke's father had a large, well-stocked dry goods store. During the German occupation he suddenly became ill and, within a few days, he was dead. Paulina hadn't even known he was so sick. When she returned the iron she had borrowed from Devorah, she came unexpectedly upon loud crying. The doctor never even said what the patient died of. He was a weak man, lay down, and never got up again. The shop was closed during the occupation and Devorah slowly sold off the merchandise. She lived on whatever she could salvage of the store's fabrics, slowly acquired new remnants of materials, ready-made dresses, anything that came to hand. Eventually, she went into business and became a peddler: bought, sold. During the occupation, when the German mark was cheap and money lost its value, Devorah earned quite well. The bigger and smaller bourgeoisie who fled during the war began to come back. All were ragged and tattered. The houses had been destroyed, industry was at a standstill. She earned money selling dresses, furniture, linens. The long years of wandering in foreign places made people yearn to have their own homes, their own things, everything that gave the illusion of their former quiet, normal lives.

Devorah kept a maid. Yoshke went to school. But then the currency stabilization put an end to her business. Instead of old-fashioned furniture with faded embroidered pillows, instead of real metal samovars and fine jewelry, Devorah now deals in rags the city's impoverished people sold in the market. She has long since let the maid go. She has been robbed twice. Yoshke no longer goes to school. When his mother goes out to the street, he sits at home and guards the house. He is more interested in watching the games on the playing field than in anything else. Yoshke wants to be strong so as not to fear anyone. And he likes going to the theater. Yoshke goes to every single show in the Yiddish theater. As soon as his mother comes home, he vanishes. It's not the performance itself that most interests him, it's the trick of getting into the theater without a ticket. The next day, the windowpanes rattle with his voice and the entire courtyard hears how he got into the theater and managed to sit in the second row, like a nobleman.

During my first summer living in the courtyard, I tried to protest

against the redhead's yelling, but I soon understood the boy was pro-
tected by a certain sympathy all the neighbors showed him.

"Yoshke," a mother hurrying with her basket to the marketplace
would implore. "Yoshke, look, keep an eye on my Leibele so the boys
don't kill him. And don't, God forbid, let him run to the well."

Yoshke will lean out of the window and watch the children in the
courtyard. The minute a fight breaks out, Yoshke runs down and sep-
arates them. Then, someone is likely to get hit, but even the mothers
shrug their shoulders and say nothing. The courtyard acknowledges the
authority of the boy with the heavy fists and laughing eyes.

Today Paulina does not stop talking. Now she takes Dante's bronze
mask down from the wall and wipes dust off the old poet's face.

"Who has energy for that red-haired one? But it must be said he's
a good boy. As soon as he sees how difficult it is for me to carry the
bucket, he grabs it from me and brings water to my door. But obeying
what he's told to do is not for him. I've told him many times to speak
a little more quietly and he answers that he's not yelling, he just has
good lungs. He wants to join a sports club and a sportsman must have
strong lungs."

Dante's mask is back in its place. With the dust cloth in her hand,
Paulina turns to me.

"What does it mean to be a sportsman?"

I explain: developing the body, gymnastics, exercises.

She wonders, "Isn't Yoshke strong?"

The holes in my socks are mended. The rain has stopped. I'm in a
hurry and want to cut the conversation short. "A sportsman is like . . .
a *sokol*, a member of the Polish Falcon Gymnastics Club." Paulina is
amazed. "Jews can also be *sokols?*" I see that she doesn't understand. She
lowers her head and is silent and I see she doesn't believe it, no, that
can't be true. She has been living for twenty-eight years among Jews,
but this just doesn't make sense. I put on my hat and see her pensive
face in the mirror. I smile. Actually, she's right, that old Paulina: a Jew

will never become a Falcon. No, not that. A Jew can become strong, but he won't be able to take pride in his fists. No, definitely not.

# V

In the low wooden house near my window the paralyzed Jew lives with his pretty, quiet daughter. He had been a wood merchant, quite a rich one. A few years ago, in winter, he was traveling with a driver to look at a forest on a piece of land being sold by a well-known landowner. Driving back to the station, the driver and he got lost. The short winter day ended. It was dark. The two Jews drove around for a few hours until a clear, starry night descended over the woods. The frost was piercing and the tired horse fell into a snowdrift almost up to its neck. With great difficulty, the men dragged it out of the snow. The horse shivered in all its bones and remained standing under a large fir tree. Branches covered in snow stretched over the weary men like angry hands. The stars looked far away and unfamiliar as they gleamed and blazed in the dark sky. Very far, very unfamiliar.

In the morning, a few woodcutters noticed the snowed-under sleigh. The station was not far, and they rescued the half-frozen people, but the merchant's legs were paralyzed. They hung like two sticks and the healthy, not-at-all old widower who had been about to marry again, remained a cripple. His wealth melted away: doctors, cures, spas. His son, who now directed the business and provided him with living expenses, had gotten married a year ago to a rich orphan from a small shtetl.

The cripple, the father, moved to our courtyard because it has a ground floor apartment. When the weather is good, his daughter takes him outside in his wheelchair and he sits in front of the building. Here is where the tall Jew with his straight, broad back and nice black beard sits. Only at his temples has his hair become a bit gray. A pair of flashing black eyes shine in his fresh, reddish face—a strong man, a neat and dapper one. His large white hands lie on his knees or pull impatiently at the fringes of the heavy shawl covering his immobile, sickly legs. He has had bad luck. And not just he: his pale, pretty daughter takes care of her father all day long, cooking, washing, and keeping the house clean. She had been about to finish school. The widower wanted to find her a husband, especially since he himself was thinking of marrying again, but the tragedy upset all his plans.

Sometimes his son and daughter-in-law come from town. Everything about her is long and pointy: a long, pointy nose, pointy shoulders, long, thin arms, pointy eyes. She is the most important, rich, and fashionable woman in their shtetl.

Today, from my place at my desk, I see her sitting in front of the house on a bench near her father-in-law. She sways back and forth, never taking her eyes off her new, pointy yellow shoes, and telling stories: this year she added an addition to her house, a glass greenhouse facing the street, no worse than her Uncle Isaac's, who thinks so much of himself because of his balcony. Let the people in town see how respectable people live. When she was a girl, she never thought she would remain in a small shtetl, she says in her shrill voice. She had been offered a match with an assistant pharmacist in Grodno, but then, when she was left an orphan, she couldn't be too picky.

The cripple moves about restlessly, his piercing black eyes looking at the woman's face, gliding down her angular, flat figure. His full, red lips grimace. He has seen better in his life. Sighing, he turns away. His daughter-in-law does not stop talking.

If God grants that her business prospers this year, she will see to it that her sister-in-law gets married.

She turns to the girl who is standing in the open doorway. The girl's pale cheeks turn red. She lowers her head. Her white, freshly washed dress fits her quite well. Meanwhile, the son unpacks a basket. He is a tall young man wearing a striped shirt and a watch. The couple have brought his father a sack of flour, a pot of butter, and a container of pickled cucumbers grown in their own garden. A sack is tied to the basket. The young man opens it, takes out a large fish and carries it over to his father. The paralyzed Jew examines the gift with great interest and shakes his head. "Such a pike—big as a lion." The sad girl goes over to him. His daughter-in-law gets up from the bench, her hands on her hips. Everyone is standing around the chair looking at the fish. A happy smile smooths out the wrinkles on the cripple's forehead. For a very brief moment life is good even here. Life.

# VI

On the different floors of our building live merchants, storekeepers, owners of small businesses, an insurance salesman, a midwife with a daughter who is a student. There are no rich people, but even in the difficult years of the German occupation, no one hungered here. Now things are worse. The stores are empty. The Jews are, for the most part, déclassé.

That's how it happened that Khatsye, the coachman, is now the most well-off Jew in our courtyard. He has a large, airy apartment on the ground floor and a stable big enough for three horses. Khatsye is not young, but he is a healthy man, as strong and straight as an old tree, and he carries his sixty years very lightly. His face is sunburned and hardened from the sun and wind. He is the ringleader of the coachmen and he doesn't hesitate to do a favor if the occasion presents itself. His son, an only child, resembles his father, but is thin and lean, with white teeth shining under his dark moustache.

Moyshe, Khatsye's son, is still quite young. When he leaves the stable and sits on the droshky in fine clothes with sparkling buttons and a hat pulled down over his brooding eyes, he looks like a young nobleman. He rides out onto the street very quickly. The minute he lifts the whip, the horse pulls the light wagon through the gate. As soon as the young coachman harnesses the horse and leads it out of the stable, girls go out to the courtyard. Just then is when they have to run to the store, or down to the cellar to get something or put something away. Or maybe they just want to stand outside for a while. But Khatsye's son pays no attention to women. When they start up with him, he blushes a little and looks away. It's clear he was raised holding onto his mother's apron strings. She gave birth to five children, but he was the only one who lived. An overprotected child, this was his first year helping his father. Until a little while ago Khatsye employed a boy, but this year his twenty-year-old son drives in the afternoons. I often see him standing at his place on the corner of the street in the line of droshkies. He is a nice looking, polite young man.

As I passed by Moyshe one evening, I noticed he was talking to the young woman who sells vegetables and soda-water from a table near the spice store. When I turned my head a little later, I saw the young coachman standing in front of the table, his hat to one side and his dark hair fallen onto his forehead. The fully grown, slightly pockmarked girl handed him a glass of cold, fizzy seltzer. Her frightened glance seemed welded to his face. Another time, I saw Khatsye's son accompanying the girl from the railway station with a few boxes of merchandise and later—it was already winter—Moyshe's mother found out about the girl. At the marketplace, a woman said to her, "It's true she's a good girl, hardworking and has some money, but how does she come to Khatsye's only son? She's an old maid, almost old enough to be his mother."

But the news came too late. On the previous evening, when the girl was cleaning off her table and had carried her merchandise into the store, Moyshe's sleigh arrived. The young coachman was in a good mood. He had a good day driving an American visitor. Every now and then they would stop to visit some establishment, a synagogue, and so on. A Vilna Jew whom Moyshe knew well was traveling with the foreigner. They stopped for a particularly long time near the courtyard of the Great Synagogue. The young coachman was very familiar with the customs followed by such visitors. It wasn't the first time he'd driven them around. As soon as they start touring the city, they ask to be taken first to the narrow ghetto streets. They have him stop at the old Jewish houses. The foreign guests pay well for that, so today he earned quite a lot.

When the shopkeeper stops and says good evening, he tells her about his guest and that he had stood still more than driven. His horse isn't even tired.

"Come sit here, Reyzele, let's drive a bit, there are wonderful paths."

The smiling girl stands on the sidewalk and blushes.

"Come, Reyzele, sit here!"

There she is, sitting in the sleigh, her knees covered with a good fur blanket with blue fringes. The sleigh begins to slide. Soon they drive onto a wide, noisy street. It is bright as day. Advertisements and colorful placards blaze; restaurants and movie theaters throw beams of light onto the street; red and green bottles sparkle like rubies and emeralds in the pharmacy's window. Cars fly by, sleigh bells ring, people huddled in their coats crowd the sidewalks. Women hide their frozen cheeks in their high, fur collars and look around happily.

Reyzele is rarely on this big street. She hides her hands in her sleeves, raises her narrow collar, and looks around. She is a bit confused by the noise, but they soon drive to a small street and to the bridge over the frozen lake. The coachman holds the reins, urging the horse to run faster and faster. They are soon past the city. On one side stretch long fences, on the other side are white fields. Here and there is a tree dressed in a snowy lace cloak. The full round moon is covered in a thin, silvery veil and there, where its light does not reach, stretch deep blue shadows on the white ground. From up high, large stars sparkle and flitter.

The girl sits behind the young coachman. Her heart is beating, her cheeks aflame from the frost and excitement. She feels as if she is flying high above the ground, and, as if in a dream, her whole life flies with her. In front of her eyes the reel of her poor, narrow life unravels, one picture after another: her childhood in the little store in the market-place, the death of her mother—her lovely, joyful mother—long years of poverty and loneliness. Her stepfather, the hunchbacked synagogue caretaker, is the young orphan's only friend in the world. He remarried soon after her mother's death. His second wife brought him a slew of children, but he never forgot the little girl, the daughter of his first, truly beloved wife.

The reel of Reyzele's past spins further: before her, like a pale shadow, stands the shtetl boy to whom her mother's friend betrothed her. When the war broke out she accompanied him to the railroad station. A group of soldiers were pushing themselves onto the railroad cars. The soldiers were yelling, singing, playing harmonicas. After all, they were going to chase away the enemy. Reyzele never saw her fiancé again. Lost, disappeared forever.

The German occupation brought fear, hunger, people dropping in the streets. Reyzele had a roof over her head: fleeing neighbors let her into their home so she could watch over their belongings. But there was nothing to eat. Reyzele carried sacks of potatoes or beets from the neighboring villages on her back, traded an old tablecloth for a loaf of bread, a silver Russian coin for some groats or a little flour. The Germans caught her more than once. The girl sat in prison more than once. She barely managed to get out, crying, cursing, freed—and once again wandering around. She smuggled saccharine, did laundry, cleaned the homes of German officers, bartered with the same people who had arrested her. She earned, saved every cent thinking of only one thing: to become somebody, to live respectably. So many women, young and old, wandered the streets, but they all had someone, a father, a brother, a husband. She would see them on Sabbath afternoons walking with their husbands, a child at their side, but she, Reyzele, was alone, lonely as a stone, the only one fated to have no one. And Reyzele kept saving her money. She accumulated eight thousand rubles, real Czar Nicholas rubles. She exchanged them for new bills—denominations of five hundreds.

The sleigh flies and the girl's thoughts fly with it. The Germans left, others came, unrest followed. Drunken soldiers wandered through the town, robbing, shooting. Reyzele buried her treasure in a corner of the cellar under broken barrels. And she kept on working, waiting for quieter times.

One day, her stepfather said, "Russian currency keeps falling. Do something with your money. Trade for dollars."

The sleigh flies. The young coachman sits in front of her and the past chases her from behind. Black clouds tear through the silver veil covering the moon. It grows dark. The girl's whole body shivers.

The sun had not yet set the day she went down to the cellar, moved away the barrel, and began to dig. A bit of light on the ground threw long shadows on the damp walls. Reyzele pushed the shovel into the earth, seeking, seeking. Where was the box? A cold sweat poured down her forehead. Finally, she heard a weak clang. The shovel had found something. Reyzele pulled on the lid of the box. The wood fell apart, and in her hands remained a narrow piece with black letters: "Havana Cigars." Also lying there was a long gold chain she had gotten by trading saccharine. The brown box she had kept since the time of the Germans, the cache of banknotes—all rotted, nothing more than a pile of soft, wet garbage. Reyzele couldn't remember how she got out of the cellar. Once she was home, the girl fainted.

Since that dreadful hour, the fear in her eyes has never gone away.

The sleigh goes further. Hot tears pour over Reyzele's face. She cannot stop them. They just keep pouring. Moyshe, the coachman turns around.

"What is it, Reyzele?" He looks at her. "Why are you crying?" He jumps over to her side and, still holding the reins in his hand, he sits next to her. "What is it?" The sleigh turns, her head falls onto his shoulder. She covers her face with her hands and cries loudly. The young coachman embraces her. "Don't cry." He grimaces like a child who has been wronged. The girl presses closer to him. He feels her soft, warm bosom under his arms.

"Don't cry, Reyzele, don't cry. We'll get married. Do you hear, Reyzele!" The girl trembles.

"This is thanks to what my mother has merited in heaven," she murmurs.

Khatsye the coachman's small, round wife, is walking around the room.

"How did we get to such a match? Who is her family? An old maid. She could be his mother."

She glances at the mirror on the dresser. Khatsye is standing at the large, tiled stove getting ready for work. He is wearing a fur coat. His cloth coat is hanging near the door. On his head he has a beaver hat with a velvet brim. He does not yet want to replace the good fur hat he has held onto since the time of the Russians. He has just come from the stable and is warming his hands.

"Well, she does have dollars," Khatsye says, and is quiet for a bit. "Look to it, my wife, that our son will have nothing to regret." And he looks at his watch. Both sigh.

The young coachman is uneasy, brooding. After a few days, the girl's stepfather, the hunchback, arrives. He says that although Reyzele is an orphan, without a father or mother, she left five hundred dollars with the rabbi, as well as gold and silver and fine household goods she earned with her own labor. God has blessed Khatsye with a son, the youngest of five children and the only one still living. "One must not humiliate an orphan," says the hunchback.

The courtyard is in an uproar. Paulina tells me that on Saturday afternoon the bride and her stepfather, the little Jew with the crooked body, came to Khatsye the coachman. The bride wore a fine velvet coat and a long gold chain that reached to her knees. Paulina went over there in the evening and saw the chain through the window. The bride was not pretty. Nor was she young. Another in her place would not have taken such a handsome young man. That's what the entire courtyard says. Such a boy, such a foolish boy, can be convinced of anything, and for money one can have anything one wants. If she, Paulina, had money, she would be able to marry even now. Well, we will soon see what comes of all this.

It is Passover. It is late in the day and the sun shines down, gentle and friendly. The sun's rays play tag in my room, running around on the floor, clambering on the walls. Lively sunlight brightens the golden frames of the pictures and Dante's bronze mask suddenly seems to smile. People are impatient. Their blood flows more quickly in their veins, an expectation of some sort quickens their pulse and animates their eyes.

In our courtyard the snow grows dark and Yulke, the caretaker, shovels it into piles. In the middle of the courtyard the warm rays of the sun are mirrored in small, thin rivulets. The peddler's boy comes home from school. He stops, takes a metal-bladed skate out of his bag, binds it to his right foot, and starts to slide on the small strip near the wall where the sun does not reach and the ice is still hard.

Near the coachman's door a rope is strung from one wall of the courtyard to the opposite wall. Reyzele is airing out her things: a pair of red quilts, a fancy tablecloth, her husband's winter clothes. She stands near the door and watches over her things. Her face has grown paler and the fear in her eyes has disappeared. The first warm breeze shakes the fine embroidered quilts and plays with Reyzele's thick brown hair. In the courtyard, near a mound of wet snow, stands the caretaker. She leans on her shovel and looks dreamily off into the distance. A gentle breeze wafts over her weathered face and awakens memories of what has passed, what will never return, but what surely once was.

# VII

It hisses, it hums, it whistles. What is this? A snake? An airplane descending onto our courtyard? Alarmed, I go to the open window and look out. Yoshke is standing on the opposite side. He is holding both hands in front of his face as if he is playing a trumpet and his mouth emits muffled whistling sounds. I understand: this means Paulina has asked him not to yell so much, so Yoshke has begun to whistle in order not to disturb me. I start waving to him with both hands: "Enough, enough." We look at one another and both of us start laughing. Yoshke is embarrassed and runs away from the window. The red lock of hair has gone into hiding. The children playing in the courtyard are also frightened by the whistling. They raise their heads and run away. But Big Mirele—she is already ten years old—calls them back. There is a smaller Mirele in our courtyard. Big Mirele is afraid of nothing so she continues with the game of blind man's bluff. Mankl, Yulke's daughter, plays with her. She has braided a green ribbon into her hair and she runs around tripping because of her big, long dress, made from an old undergarment of her mother's. A blindfolded boy chases after the children. They run away from him. He catches Mirele by the arm, but the quick girl wants to free herself. The boy holds onto her, will not let her go. She hits him over the head. That's what Mirele always does. She doesn't much care: a wallop here, a wallop there. She does not shy away from striking a blow. The boy rips off his blindfold and bursts into tears. The children take his side: Mirele doesn't play fair. Big Mirele hits. There is a big commotion.

Yoshke appears at the window. The situation is clear. Yoshke runs down into the courtyard. "Listen, I'll make you pay for this so once and for all you'll remember what it means to hit people." He rolls up his sleeves. Mirele looks up and does not budge from her spot. Only her thick black eyebrows show any sign of movement.

"All right, so let's have it. Go ahead," she calls out and looks him right in the eye. "Well. Well." The large, raised fist is lowered. The boy turns away. Mirele bends one knee and springs away on one foot like a stork. "Let's play," she calls out, as if nothing has happened. Yoshke shakes his head and goes back upstairs. This pretty girl who jumps around like a stork is not at all afraid of Yoshke.

Reyzele the storekeeper appears in the doorway. She can barely walk. Slowly and carefully she drags her big body. She holds her head up high. The cripple's quiet daughter is standing on the threshold of her home. Thoughtfully, she looks at the shapeless form of the pregnant young woman.

Khatsye the coachman's daughter-in-law gives birth to a girl. The labor was difficult and she had to be taken to the hospital. The doctors advised her to stay in the hospital, but she wanted to go home as soon as possible. Paulina thinks Reyzele was missing her husband. Paulina is an old maid. She is jealous.

Reyzele is home already. She cannot produce enough milk to nurse the baby. The newborn was given to a wet nurse. Today, Reyzele is sitting at the window and the young coachman is standing nearby, at the stable. He is talking to our young lady, the student. Another student, a young man, is also standing there, holding a thin stick with which he hits the grass growing near the wall. The young people hire a droshky for a trip out of town. They will have clothing and food in the wagon. Most of the students will walk, says our young lady. She is amused. The new maid is running across the courtyard. She has recently come to work for one of the neighbors. She stops and looks around. She is wearing new shoes on her bare feet and her eyes shine. The sick young woman at the window grows paler. She does not take her frightened eyes off her husband.

Reyzele the storekeeper is ill. I saw them take her back to the hospital. She sat on the freshly polished droshky, leaning on her mother-in-law, and in front of her sat her husband, the young coachman.

At my side now sits the peddler, Yoshke's mother. She takes a letter out of her pocket and shows it to me. I know her youngest brother got in touch with her a few years ago, after he had not been heard from since the war. Things were not going well for him and he had been unable to find a place for himself for a long time. Now he writes that he has been in a settlement in Palestine for the last two years and he and his wife are working the land. He writes he is planning to bring over his nephew, Yoshke, soon.

"But when will that be? Meanwhile, the boy is going to seed here," sighs Devorah. "And what will become of me?"

I calm her down. "You'll see, Devorah, your brother and Yoshke will bring you to them in due time. Yoshke is a good boy. You know him."

Devorah turns away and wipes her eyes with her handkerchief.

After a while, I ask, "How is the young coachman's wife?" Devorah tells me Reyzele is back home. The family had to bring the sick woman home because she refused to stay in the hospital any longer. Devorah went to find out why she hadn't remained in the hospital and chided her for not waiting until she was well. It is better to be treated in a hospital than at home where you cannot be cured. What good are the quacks who come to her at home? What good is that drunkard who feeds her blades of grass and cheats her out of her money? The young woman, silent and frightened, looked away. But Devorah saw how sick she was so she wouldn't leave it alone and tried to convince her to listen to the doctors.

"I can't leave my husband alone. I have to guard my treasure," Reyzele finally said and turned to the wall.

"Reyzele is afraid to leave her treasure alone," says Devorah and stands up. There is a slight smile on her face, a half ironic, half sad smile of a woman who has already played out the bittersweet game of love and joy.

Reyzele the storekeeper dies. There is a large funeral. All the neighbors stand in the courtyard. The crippled merchant sits near the door in his wheelchair. The children gather in a corner of the courtyard. Dumbfounded, Moyshe stares at the wagon taking away his wife, who had come to our courtyard just a short time ago with such joy and hopefulness. Now she is lying in a box, and behind her walks the young coachman who brought her here.

It is raining a little and the broken red bricks on the wall look like dried blood. The recently married young man walks with a bowed head and grimaces like a wronged child. The little hunchback limps after him.

# VIII

Autumn. The low-hanging sun throws down short, pointy shadows. The air is cold and clean. The horizon is far and wide.

Piles of vegetables lie in the marketplace. Red tomatoes shine near white cauliflower with velvety tops. Wine-red beets are strewn across the tables, light brown potatoes pour out of sacks, yellow carrots push their pointy thin tips out of baskets, off to one side hard, misshapen radishes, white ones and bluish ones push forward, heaps of peas lie in boxes. The delicate young peas are hiding in their thin pods. Piles of cucumbers attract the eye.

Peddlers with bound feet hurry everywhere. Foolish ducks waddle on their short legs and their large, hungry beaks quack. A barefoot gentile boy roams around. Under his arm he is holding a long fishing rod, three times as big as him, and in his hand, on a string, a few small pike fish are wriggling. The narrow pathways are covered with husks and vegetable peels. A peasant sits on an unhitched wagon and plays a sad tune on his harmonica. Children chase after a big shaggy dog. A tall, thin woman smooths out the deep creases on her old, dark face and sits down on a box in front of a sack of scallions. Women stand in doorways with baskets full of apples sweet as sugar. Grownups and children chew blue, hard plums and sink their teeth into juicy green pears.

Holiday foods are already arrayed in the bakeries. There are gleaming jars of preserves and brown cakes bathed in dark, fragrant honey. The fruit stores have large watermelons with pieces cut out through which can be seen their red, sweet flesh and black, damp seeds.

There is a commotion in the streets. People bump up against one another on the sidewalks. Carts packed high with hay block the streets. The peasants yell, the coachmen take money and make change, voices ring out like bells in the crystal-clear air.

Summer is gone. Nature and people add up the results of their hard, intense labor. It is Sukkos.

In our courtyard, near the walls, lie mounds of red, green, and golden leaves that fall from the fir tree. They look like large bouquets and exude a fine, sweet smell.

Late at night, strained, sad sounds can be heard from the next courtyard. Jews are praying.

It is still light out, but I don't want to do anything. I stand near the open window and wrap myself in a warm shawl.

The cripple's wheelchair sits near his door. His daughter covers his legs with a blanket. She is standing at the threshold of their home. The last sunbeams light up her face. Her hair shines.

At Khatsye the coachman's house his little round wife is sitting on a chair. She rocks her grandchild in her arms. The baby is wrapped in

Reyzele's good shawl. She is jumping on her grandmother's knees and stretches her arms out to the wet nurse who has brought her here and is standing near the chair with empty hands. The wet nurse is a strong Jewish woman in a white kerchief tied behind her red, meaty ears. From afar, I hear both women laughing and playing with the little one.

Khatsye and Moyshe come out of their house with another Jew—a stranger. They stop near the stable. Moyshe measures the entrance. They consult, walking back and forth in the courtyard. Khatsye is striking a deal with the man about bringing goods from the train. Khatsye wants to create a business for his son. They buy a pair of expensive packhorses and rent a large warehouse. Reyzele's dollars have been put to good use.

The young man has grown broader and stronger. His face is sunburned and he bears a strong resemblance to his father. His hair falls onto his forehead. He keeps his hands in the pockets of his leather jacket.

In the building opposite mine, a window opens. Devorah has seen me. She waves a blue envelope at me and yells that she cannot leave her house. She has sent Yoshke to fetch some things; as soon as the boy comes, she will bring me the letter. But I recognize the envelope: it is a letter from her brother, and I can see Devorah is distressed about something. I am curious. I wrap myself in my warm shawl and cross the courtyard to her. Devorah is waiting for me on the stairs. We remain standing. She tells me her brother is insisting that she send his nephew. He tells them what papers the boy must prepare and he writes that he will soon send money for his fare. Devorah is upset. Her cheeks are aflame. It is clear she has been shedding tears.

—And what does Yoshke say?

—The boy is very confused. He'll soon want to turn even Fayvke into a pioneer in Palestine—smiles Devorah.—My brother writes to say I shouldn't worry; as soon as Yoshke gets used to things and begins to earn a little money, they'll send for me too. A mother can go to be with her son. They'll find some work for me too. But that's not the point—she says, lost in thought. I haven't seen my brother for so many years. My boy is a mischief maker. I don't know my sister-in-law. What will she say? Yoshke is still such a young child!

Yoshke appears at the entranceway. He is carrying a large sack on his back. His mother goes to meet him. I ask Devora for the settlement's address. She turns around and shows me the blue envelope. I go home.

Khatsye is standing near the cripple's chair. The Jews talk, the girl goes into the house, the recently widowed young man waits on the side.

Slowly, I go upstairs. Yoshke's uncle lives in the ancient land, on ground cultivated by Jewish hands, watered with Jewish sweat, built anew—a bridge between East and West built by Jewish labor, cemented with Jewish blood.

It grows dark. I close the window. It is quiet in the courtyard. People have gone their separate ways. In the rooms, behind the windowpanes, lamps are lit.

# Acknowledgments

I happened upon Chana Blankshteyn's volume of short stories during the year I spent researching women's Yiddish prose writing as the National Endowment for the Humanities Senior Fellow at the Center for Jewish History. I am grateful to the staff of both institutions for the opportunity to do the research that led to this translation, and to the librarians and archivists of CJH and the YIVO Institute who helped make that year and so many others productive. These translations were begun when I was a fellow at the University of Michigan's Frankel Institute for Advanced Judaic Studies, during a year whose theme was Yiddish Studies. The opportunity to be with such thoughtful readers and learned scholars was a gift matched only by the friendships nurtured in the halls of the South Thayer Building.

Two of Blankshteyn's stories in this volume are slightly edited versions of previous publications. "Fear" first appeared in the online journal *In geveb* in March 2020 (https://ingeveb.org/texts-and-translations/fear). "Do Not Punish Us" appeared in *Lilith* in Summer 2020.

# About the Translator

Anita Norich is Collegiate Professor Emerita of English and Judaic Studies at the University of Michigan. Her most recent book, *A Jewish Refugee in New York*, is a translation of a Yiddish novel by Kadya Molodovsky. She is also the author of *Writing in Tongues: Yiddish Translation in the Twentieth Century*, *Discovering Exile: Yiddish and Jewish American Literature in America During the Holocaust*, and *The Homeless Imagination in the Fiction of Israel Joshua Singer*. She translates Yiddish literature, and she lectures and publishes on a range of topics concerning modern Jewish cultures, Yiddish language and literature, Jewish American literature, and Holocaust literature.